The
Greatest
Parenting
Book Ever

The
Greatest
Parenting
Book Ever

HOW TO NOT FUCK UP YOUR KID

Nick
Childress

To My Kiddo-

Go get your dreams out of life.
… And don't be afraid to laugh.

Love,
Dad

What You'll Find Here…
And Where You'll Find It

CHAPTER 2

CHAPTER 3

CHAPTER 4

CHAPTER 5

CHAPTER 6

CHAPTER 7

CHAPTER 8

CHAPTER 12

CHAPTER 13

CHAPTER 14

CHAPTER 15

BONUS

Foreword

What Is This? And Who Is This For?

This is a book.
A book for adults.
A book for adults and their teenage children.
A book for adults and their teenage children who might be considering the idea of making grandparents out of previously mentioned adults.

This is a *book*.
A book written by a parent.
A book written by a parent for other parents.
A book written by a parent for soon-to-be parents.
A book written by a parent for non-parents.
A book written for non-parents who think having a child will solve their problems.

Non-parent problems.

Non-parent, childless problems.

Non-parent, childless problems like freedom, traveling the world, buying expensive clothing, eating at fancy restaurants, and drinking the night away.

Non-parent, childless problems like arguing about where to go on a spontaneous vacation, and wondering if it's possible to be with someone who thinks Fiji is the be-all, end-all vacation spot.

Or bleaker, non-parent, childless problems like filling a void post-breakup and settling on a new person who brings out a wild side. A wild side resulting in job loss and an arrest for indecent exposure at a sporting event.

Or youthful, non-parent, childless problems like being in love in high school and disenchanted with life. Problems that sound like, "Fuck it. Life is better outside the comfort of my parents' home. A home where I'm provided for. A home where I don't pay rent. A home where the most responsibility I've ever had is getting paid to take out the trash. The audacity of my parents. They're holding me back. 'Hey, Candace! Let's run away and have a family of our own. That will fix everything!'"

Those are non-parent, childless problems, and they are real. They are very real places to start the parenting journey from. If you are experiencing those problems, this book is for you.

Or if you're just normal, with routine, boring, non-parent problems, this book is for you.

Or if you think having a child will solve any other problems, this book is for you, too.

Ultimately, if you have a sense of humor and an inkling that one day you want something to do with kids, this book is for you.

WHAT ISN'T THIS? AND WHO ISN'T THIS FOR?

What isn't this? Interesting how that question doesn't work well in the negative.

What this isn't, is some childless, PhD scholar's attempt to bore you to death. This is not one of the books you pretend to read while you're in front of your parent friends. This book isn't filled with charts and graphs that try to generalize children into easily predictable groups that don't hold up in the real world.

This book isn't filled with lame advice like *The Top Ten Tips for Dealing with Tantrums*. No. It doesn't pretend to know how to get your child to shut the fuck up. It doesn't pretend to know how to get your child to calm the fuck down when they knock all the canned goods off the shelf at the grocery store.

This book doesn't pretend. It doesn't pretend to tell you that your child isn't a bratty asshole destined to destroy the world. If you are looking for denial, go somewhere else.

This book isn't G-rated either. If you're looking for the G-rated version, we have news for you: It doesn't exist.

For those of you too busy to read, an audiobook is available. You'll find it under the explicit section. It isn't bleeped out, and it isn't narrated by some boring, pathetic actor. It's narrated by a not boring, not pathetic, former actor.

This book isn't an app promising to be the newest thing to distract your kid for a few moments. It's not a book written by some socially awkward fuck named Tim, or *Timmy*, as his sole friend calls him, in a dark corner of his tenth-floor office.

No. This isn't any of that. It's so much more.

What You'll Get From This Book

This book is meant to be a starting point. A roadmap. A guide to help make sense of the plethora of bullshit that is the Baby Industry. It's meant to inspire honesty, authenticity, and candid discussion with oneself and one's social group. A social group that, upon reflection, might just be imaginary. Or it might be a very small social group. Or it might be a social group of one: you. And that's okay. Read this book and that might change ... if you do everything perfectly. No promises.

This book is written with a twinkle in the eye and a hope to challenge the current cultural climate that has polarized and paralyzed the parenting world with fear and shame.

This book will ask you to ask yourself challenging questions. It will push the envelope. But while pushing the envelope and challenging the core of a life's worth of ideals, it will ask you to be patient with yourself. After all, you're new to this ... and you don't yet know that secretly, parenting is so much simpler than most parents—and the Industry—want you to believe.

So enjoy the book. It's filled with the necessary fundamentals to not fuck up your kid's life before it starts.

Introduction

Some of you might already have little ones running around. Others might be pregnant, expecting a glorious life ahead. For both groups, this introduction and the following sections might be a shock. That's because you might never have thought about these questions or about the logistics of having kids before starting your journey.

Before addressing logistics though, you need to answer some questions. Before you answer questions, you should be clear on what the logistics of parenting are.

Logistics like: Do you have the money to support a little leech who will cause your bank account to hemorrhage money for ~~twenty years~~ the remainder of your nonsenile life?

Logistics like: How will your day-to-day life change when you have to prepare extra meals, do extra laundry, schedule bath times and play times, translate gibberish, endlessly shop, teach life lessons, do extra dishes, and take your kid out into the world with bags of crap that you think you'll need, but actually don't?

Logistics like: How do you deal with insecurities, including whether you can be a good role model and teach your child to survive in this cruel, selfish, dystopian world? A world that told you to pursue your dreams but ultimately trapped you in the hamster wheel of day-to-day life. There you are, trapped in a hamster wheel, where you work tirelessly for a meager paycheck, answering to some idiot middle manager, hoping that tomorrow your miracle will come and your golden ticket will magically appear. There you are, in denial of the reality that you've done nothing but the same routine for years and never took a chance to be noticed in this proverbial rat race, yet you still expect change.

Those are parenting logistics. At least they are in this book. They are very important logistics to address. But before you get to those logistics, there is one question to consider that rises above all others:

Should You Be A Parent?

Should you, reader of this book, be a parent?
Should *you* be a parent?
Not everyone should.
And not enough people ask that question.

Because not enough people ask that question, society gets to deal with spoiled, silver spoon–fed, entitled assholes. Society inherits the fantastic, fulfilling job of convincing full-grown adults that their parents *did* love them. That their parents were just flawed people. That forgiving them is okay. That they don't have to be like their parents. And they don't have to act out and be a jaded, apathetic hipster.

Fuck hipsters, and fuck their hipster parents. Finally, people of the world, we can agree on something.

So here you are. Should *you* be a parent?

Here are some ways to tell if you *shouldn't* be a parent:

If you'd rather spontaneously go to a grungy dive bar to do lines of cocaine off a toilet seat ... you probably shouldn't be a parent.

If you think of kids as more of a possession, an accessory, or a doll that happens to be alive, which you occasionally bring around for a photo or a holiday before sending them back to *the room you never go into* ... you probably shouldn't be a parent.

If you think that having a child will solve your problems and fill the void that you can't figure out how to fill on your own ... then, at least right now, you probably shouldn't be a parent.

It might sound harsh, but why should you have the right to create a person, only to bring them up in a shitty existence? Why should you have the right to set your future offspring up for decades of mental, physical, and emotional trauma?

If you really want to be a parent, you should start by being a parent. Put your ego to the side, think about the health of your future child, and ask yourself if you should *be* a parent.

So ... should you be a parent? If the answer is no ... give yourself some time, make the changes you need to make, and ask again later. If the answer is yes ... then get ready for a wild ride.

And ...

Congratulations!

You're about to embark upon a journey that's going to blast your life into the air like a firework and blow it up into a thousand flaming pieces of paper. After which you'll float back down to earth, not knowing which way is up or which piece goes where, and then you'll try to put it all back together.

Parenthood is a journey that exaggerates everything. A journey that will put your life in a blender, eat it for breakfast, and dispense it out ten to twelve times a day via diapers. It's such a difficult journey, that calling it a *journey* doesn't do it justice.

It's a quest! You're about to go on a quest!

Doesn't that sound like fun?

The Quest!

You are about to become Don Quixote. You've embarked upon a quest. The quest of your life. A quest to raise a family and right the wrongs of your youth. The wrongs you've been dwelling on for years.

You're going to learn from the wrongs of your own parents. Wrongs you keenly noticed as you brushed your teeth at seven years old, listening to your parents argue in the other room. You're going to remember those moments, those wrongs, and improve upon them.

You've set out on your quest to live out the fictional world of parenting that's in your head. You've set out on your quest to live out the fictional TV family life that has been dangled in front of you, like a carrot, from day one. You've set out on your quest to finally achieve the family life of your dreams. The carrot is within reach.

Though you never got to experience it during your child-hood—because your family was too busy bitching about spilled cereal and curfews—you know that the family world of your dreams will come true. It exists! You know it because every time you watch a movie, or turn on the television, or read a book, it's there in all of its happy TV family glory. That's the quest you've embarked on, and if you're like most people, you are currently convinced that you will conquer your quest for the perfect family!

Some will say the quest you've embarked on is impossible. That it's a figment of your imagination. Fuck the naysay-ers—it's only fictional in their reality, not in yours. In your reality, the dream is real! So you're going to be realistic. You're right, and they're wrong. You will not be defeated. You will have a life that looks like a modern version of *The Jetsons.* That's what family is. And because that show is the be-all, end-all of your reality, you know that parenting is great. It's easy. There will never be any problems. And you'll achieve the goal of your quest: a perfect family.

Besides, the naysayers are only a small sliver of society. All of *your* parent friends are social and have it all togeth-er. They never struggle. They have a happy, well-balanced household. They have a great, strife-free relationship, with plenty of friends. Most of your parent friends smile and tell you parenthood is the best thing ever.

Obviously, the people who say that your quest to be a perfect parent isn't possible are the real idiots. They're the awful parents of the world. Right?

Let yourself get caught up in the excitement. You're pursuing your ideal family. It's real. And it's yours!

THE EXCITEMENT!

You're gonna be a parent! A fucking parent! YES!!! Scream it from the rooftops! Yell it out the window! The excitement is almost unbearable. And if it's not, what the fuck do you want to be a parent for? Get excited! You're about to experience the best parts of humanity!

Just think—not only do you get to care for a cute-ish, screaming little blob for twenty-four hours a day, seven days a week, three hundred and sixty-five days a year, but you also get to be treated differently. People will open doors for you. Partners will bring home dinner. Friends will throw parties in your honor and drink in front of you while you open presents, sip on sparkling water with lime, and murder the cheese plate.

You see, when you become a parent, the world revolves around you, just like when you were a kid. You're about to become the center of the universe, and you will get to reap the benefits of the power of pregnancy.

The power to eat the most awful food combinations and not have to explain shit to anyone.

The power to weep during comedies and laugh during dramas and not have to explain your reaction to any asshole who so much as looks in your direction.

The power to get police escorts through traffic with three simple words: My water broke.

And you get to imagine all the possibilities for your child's life. You get to prepare to achieve *your* dreams, goals, and expectations for *their* life. You get to plot it all, without their input. Plan away—you don't need their input. Who gives a shit about what your future kid might want? You're going to plot their perfect little life. You are in charge. You're creating this family. You are the keeper of the hopes and dreams.

The Hopes And Dreams!

A firefighter? Too dangerous.
A construction worker? Ha! Never!
A doctor or a lawyer? Too cliché.
Besides, by the time your child gets into the work force, the majority of these jobs will be run by microbots and computers powered by artificial intelligence.

Your child is too good to be a doctor or lawyer. Your child will make the microbots that put doctors out of business, or they'll use AI to develop a tool to free the world of lawyers. That's status. That's who *your* child will be.

Your child will grow up to be something exciting. Armed with a STEM education, your child will take the world by storm, founding a biotech company that becomes the first trillion-dollar corporate merger.

Your child will be a linguist who travels the world, stages a coup in some oppressed country, and then becomes its leader, ultimately freeing the natives from oppression.

Your child will live out your dreams to perfection. All because of *you*. You had the foresight to plot their life for them. You told them from birth what they would be—and then, one happy, tearful day, they looked back at you and said, "Yes, I want to be that."

Your child will be fucking amazing. Statues and buildings will be built in your child's honor. All because of the work *you* did. You put in the work to plot out their life in as much detail as possible, and you controlled every aspect of it. Every detail. You never let anything like imagination, or play, or the silly notion that they themselves should learn how to be happy, confident adults, capable of accomplishing their own dreams, get in the way of you accomplishing your dream of having the perfect TV family.

You'll have it. You'll have your fantasy. Be ruthless. They'll thank you one day.

Now let's get started.

Chapter 1

WHERE TO START?

First things first: Any hopes or dreams or expectations you might have for your child will be tossed out the window as soon as they take their first step. You can be controlling, but ultimately, they won't care. Are you really going to be that asshole parent who kids rebel against generation after generation? Of course not.

You're here because you're trying to figure out how to set up your kids for success, right? You want to be a perfect parent, right? You want your kids to look back on their childhood and say, "My folks were great." Right?

So ... where do you start?

It's counterintuitive. You start by not trying to be or do anything. As soon as you try to *be* something, especially a perfect parent, you're fucked. Now that doesn't mean disengaging from your child's life. That means if you're focused on being a perfect parent instead of living in the moment, then you'll be doomed from the start.

Say this out loud: Perfect parenting is a lie.

Take it in. Live it. Love it. Take off that pressure to be perfect. You don't need the added pressure. All you need to do is try. Try your best. Be there. Engage. You are merely a version of your child, further along in the quest. It's literally a little half version of *you*. Get to know you. Your little you will see right through your façade of perfect parenting bullshit.

That's where you start. By being honest with yourself and taking off the pressure to be perfect. Now, get ready for the ride.

By the way—here's a little secret: Raising healthy kids is pretty simple. It's hard, but simple. You'll get a lot of information that unnecessarily complicates your quest. Information that might lead you astray. Don't buy the bullshit.

INFORMATION OVERLOAD

You're going to get a lot of information. *A lot* of information. Some of that information is going to scare you. Some of it will shame you. Some of it will confuse you. Some of it will convince you that by following this program or that, you'll achieve the perfection you're looking for.

You'll hear opinions from friends and teachers, parents and priests, celebrities and gurus, and sometimes celebrity gurus, all of whom will give you conflicting information. They'll give you more books to read, classes to take, and documentaries to watch. Their underlying message: Do it my way or your kid will suffer. If you don't do it my way, you'll be doomed for eternity to be the face of *The Worst Parent Ever* magazine.

It's hard not to think, when getting bombarded with everything, "Am I already a bad parent?" You'll rush out to buy the newly suggested book. You'll research. You'll discover half of the baby products you already purchased need to be thrown away. They're poison. You'll learn *that* from the latest late-night baby product infomercial that you had on as white noise while you were reading. You'll panic and decide to start over. Then you'll buy all the products from the newest book and infomercial. Crisis averted.

You'll be buying it, all right ... hook, line, and sinker. Peer pressure is a motherfucker. Why? Because it triggers FOFUYCL, or Fear of Fucking Up Your Child's Life.

The latest book you read will promise solutions. It'll promise to lead you down the stressful, high-pressure path of positive, perfect parenting. It's basically a religion. Follow every rule, suggestion, and tenet to achieve enlightenment. Follow it perfectly, and you'll end up with the perfect family you've always dreamed of.

Until the next friend, doctor, or expert suggests something different, which will trigger you to doubt yourself and start the cycle all over again.

Well, congratulations—the cycle is over. From now on, the only parenting book you'll need is this one, where we don't offer solutions—we just point things out and make fun of them. And sometimes cry. A lot. Every day. Get rid of your gym membership, you're about to exercise the fuck out of your tear ducts.

There Is So Much Shit To Buy

You'll quickly notice that there is *so much shit to buy*. Everywhere you turn, someone is telling you that x product saved their lives. They tell you x product is responsible for their child's success.

You'll catch yourself thinking, "How did the parents of yesteryear survive without dual-pump technology? How did they function without animal-shaped, glow-in-the-dark bathtubs? Ugh. They were so deprived."

The parents of yesteryear were so primitive.

You'll continue thinking, "I read on a blog that my child's development hinges on the proper use of a natural sea sponge at bath time. I must wash my child with a sea sponge from the Great Barrier Reef, soaked in ninety-two-degree water, on the third full moon of their first year of life. Then and only then will my child succeed in living out my dreams."

You know it's true, too—you heard about the sea sponge bath theory from your favorite celebrity guru, who read about it on a ~~conspiracy theory~~ alternative parenting website.

But sea sponges aren't all you have to buy for the latest theories to work. There are the ostrich-feather pillows; the organic, bamboo crib; the grass-fed, organic, free-range, cotton sheets; the two-phase, triple-nozzle, expression tech breast pump, so you and your partner can bond while pumping; the high-definition, LED crib activity set; the BPA-free ... everything—at least, *this* week. Also, you wouldn't dare forget about the sheepskin, vibrating mattress pad; the stroller that charges your phone, warms your coffee, and will even tell you if you forgot your baby, all powered by strolling it around; a rocking chair that glides—they must never rock; bottles, spoons, nipples, and containers, all of which must be sterilized or your child will die of whatever epidemic is trending; outfits; rags; wipes; and of course, diapers—are you going to go with cloth or biodegradable? The brand names are filling up our landfills, you wouldn't dare consider those, would you?

The list goes on and on. It's never ending. And all of it must be purchased new. New products are the only way to produce a successful child. Hand-me-downs are never considered.

And why would you? Your child deserves the best. Nothing but the best. They deserve it all. Everything.

What about you? You need it all, too. Every product is a help. Perfect parenting is as simple as buying the right products. How do you know if it's the perfect product? You buy what you watched on an infomercial, what you read on your favorite website, what you discovered while reading the latest book that was suggested by that random person at the coffee shop. Surely you don't want to figure it out on your own. Surely you don't want to say to all those well-intentioned, incredibly helpful corporations, celebrities, and coffee shop people, "Thanks, but no thanks."

What kind of person would spit in the face of commercialism?

Baby Necessities

You'll get a lot of pushback when you turn your back on the Baby Industry. It'll be hard to pull away. What'll make it even harder is when the Industry puts on the hard sell and brings in your friends. You'll get a lot of, "Don't you want the best for your child?"

You do, but you've seen the light. You don't know where you're headed, but it's somewhere else. While you walk away from the fake notion of perfect, positive parenting, you might ponder, "What are the baby necessities?"

This book doesn't have the answers, because that's ultimately for you to decide. There are a few givens, though.

You'll need a safe place for the kid to sleep. *Safe* doesn't mean Fort Knox or some sterile chemistry lab. But *safe*—ya know, not a recalled death trap.

You'll need a stroller of some sort, but it doesn't need to charge your phone, warm your coffee, or match the car you're driving.

You'll need blankets, towels, and clothing; diapers, rash cream, and wipes; bottles, milk, and formula.

And love. Obviously.

Babies need love all day and all night. When you have help and when you don't. When you are tired and when you're energetic. When you know why your baby is crying and when you're flying by the seat of your pants trying to figure out why. They need love.

Love ... and the basics. Those basics can be hand-me-downs, if you're inclined. Kids grow up so fast; most hand-me-downs were worn once, maybe twice. Not the diapers and breast milk, of course. Don't fall for the industry hype. Follow the rule of KISS: Keep It Simple, Stupid. Save your money. Put it toward school. Kids born now are going to need a PhD just to get a job at a local fast food joint. They'll need all the help they can get.

Opinions Are Like Assholes

Right now, you're probably thinking, "But Sally at the salon said I need to read such and such, and buy this gadget and that gadget."

Fuck that.

There are two questions you need to ask yourself before you let Sally from the salon plant another idea in your head. Two questions you can use as the litmus test to figure out whether you want to listen to Sally at the salon with the awful haircut, who dominates your inner monologue.

Question one: Do I like Sally at the salon's child?

If the answer is no, then why are you giving so much weight to what she says? Or what the latest suggested book says? Why do you care, if you think the child is a snotty, entitled brat who is going to ruin the world?

If the answer is yes, then proceed to question two.

Question two: Who raised Sally at the salon's kid? If the kid is well-behaved, but there is a full-time, 24/7, live-in caretaker, then maybe the caretaker is the person you should talk to. Sally at the salon probably has no idea that the caretaker doesn't do the majority of what she's proselytizing to you.

Opinions are like assholes. And assholes have opinions to feel better about their shitty life.

THE FEAR OF FUCKING UP YOUR CHILD'S LIFE

"But I have to follow the crowd. I don't want to be different. I don't want to risk ruining my child's life."

Those thoughts are powerful. That fear is all consuming. That's why the Baby Industry uses it. That fear will eat you alive if you don't put a stop to it. A little drop of FOFUYCL and you'll do just about anything. The Baby Industry will back up claims with convincing studies. Studies you'll never read, just like the Terms and Agreements that give tech companies the rights to your life. Studies that make you feel confused and overwhelmed. At that point, they'll pounce. They'll trigger FOFUYCL, give you a solution, and you'll run back to them over and over again. They'll win you for life.

Everyone wants a roadmap. A definitive path. That's the problem with having information at our fingertips. Because of instant gratification, our society never learns how to live with uncertainty. Uncertainty is viewed as bad, or negative, or inefficient. Uncertainty isn't bad. It's a natural part of the new and unique.

Raising a child is the most unique process you'll ever go through in life. No one knows your child better than you do. Trust in that. Trust that you'll know your child better than anyone else in the world does. Don't let the Baby Industry or some asshole at the coffee shop tell you otherwise.

Unless of course, you plan to never be with your child, in which case, thanks in advance for giving the world another winner ...

What Kind Of Person Do You Want Your Child To Be?

"I thought the idea was to not control them to the nth degree ... "

You're right. But you still have the responsibility of raising your kid. So you have to ask the question: What kind of person do you want your child to be?

More specifically: Do you want your child to grow up to be an independent person who doesn't have to take *adulting* classes? Or do you want your child to just grow bigger and always be a child, a proverbial Peter Pan, ready to roam the streets, drunk and in a onesie Santa Claus costume?

If that's what you want your child to be, that's fine. Regardless, it's a question you need to answer for yourself.

Wouldn't you like to think that in the case of a zombie apocalypse, or a robot apocalypse, or just *the* apocalypse, your child would be enough of an adult-ish person to figure out they need to run? You don't want your child to stand there and wait to be told to run from the robot, or even worse, wait for permission to run when the zombies are coming for them, do you?

No, definitely not. You want them to figure some shit out. You want them to be an actual person. An independent person who understands that Dwayne Johnson won't always be there to save them.

In all seriousness, though, do you want your child to grow up to be self-sufficient and capable of handling the twists and turns that life throws at them? Or do you want your child to grow up to be a master of the question, "What do I do now?"

If you want the latter, there is nothing for you here.

If you want the former, then you must find the magical balance. The balance between a helping hand and a degree from The School of Hard Knocks.

A Helping Hand
Vs. The School Of Hard Knocks

This magical balance is hard to find. You'll struggle to find it every day. Every time your kid tries something new, you'll desperately try to find it. You'll ask where it is every time your child tests their limits, pushing their boundaries further and further. You'll ask where it is while you fend off evil stares and looks of judgment from strangers. You'll ask where it is when you let your kid take a risk and get a tongue lashing from some outspoken asshole who thinks you actually give a fuck what they think.

Except, deep down, you do care. Deep down, you're still trying to be the perfect parent. You care what they think. You care that your parenting triggers the judgment of others.

To top it off, you have no comeback. You won't have mastered the smug smile, the head nod of judgment, or the passive-aggressive, witty comeback. A comeback so snarky it'll stop hipsters in their tracks. A comeback like, "Thank you for your highly sought-after opinion. Your child is *so* well behaved. He must get it from you."

If you had that mastered, then the judgmental strangers of the world would roll their eyes, flip you off, and leave you alone. But you're not there—yet. You're still trying to find that magical, sweet balance between help and struggle. All while you constantly question your ability to raise a little person.

The struggle is real.

Where is the magical balance between turning your house into one big, padded room and watching your kid bust their head on a table?

Where is the magical balance between handholding and watching your child fall down the stairs after they dangled off the railing, resulting in two broken teeth and a mild concussion?

Where is the magical balance between letting them fail a test, dooming them to a mediocre existence, and helping them with homework so they can get a good grade? And that will happen ... you will *help*. Especially if you were from a family that felt a B+ was equal to an F.

The hardest part about this magical balance is that, as you watch them struggle through life, your FOFUYCL will kick in. And why wouldn't it? They're half you!

You want them to have a chance at a good school, right? Of course you do—what kind of parent wouldn't?

You want them to land a great job because of ~~nepotism~~ their strong networking skills, right? Of course you do— that's why socialization at a good school is so important.

You want them to ultimately dominate the world, right? Hell, yeah! Of course you do—the first modern ~~king~~ president of the world is sitting on your floor drooling right now.

But you're only human, and that need to help will become something else. Something dark. Something that will threaten to derail you from your quest. You'll become obsessed with perfection. You'll become ruthless, editing the fuck out of their fourth-grade essays. Turning five hundred words of "My Spring Break Vacation" into an autobiographical novel worthy of direct admittance to an Ivy League school. With your help, your child will be a prodigy. A modern-day version of Doogie Howser.

Yet, the more you help your child, the more help they'll need. It's a vicious cycle. Because of your help, they will learn nothing more than how to depend on Mommy and Daddy.

On the other side of the coin is the School of Hard Knocks. In that school, you let them fall down the steps, or fail that class, or touch the stovetop burner. They won't do that shit again. And if they do, well... college isn't for everyone.

Assume your child is average. They'll learn what to do and what not to do from their mistakes. They'll also have a visceral understanding of overcoming struggle. They'll be half Annie, half Jay-Z: intelligent, street smart, sassy, and able to connect with their future ~~subjects~~ colleagues.

Yes, your child will have trauma from all of the life lessons, but it'll be a healthy trauma. Character-building trauma. And because they'll have so much practice dealing with their trauma, they'll also know how to deal with the trauma of others.

So what? Your child might eat out a lot because they have a fear of kitchens due to knives, ovens, and hot water, but they'll be able to connect and hold a great conversation. In the School of Hard Knocks they will fail hard and will have learned the lessons only learnable by getting knocked the fuck out.

When they graduate from the School of Hard Knocks, nothing will be able to stop them. Not even a freight train, because they will have learned from their time as a child that getting hit in the face with a locomotive hurts.

Thus, a life-sized locomotive will hurt even more. That's the School of Hard Knocks in action.

But alas, no lesson is worth learning if there is no take-away. If a lesson doesn't better prepare your kid to make it in the dystopian future foretold in the cinematic arts, then it isn't worthwhile. There's no need to let them cut open their hand slicing organic bananas. Actually, that's a bad example. You don't have to worry that your child will cut their hand slicing organic bananas because organic bananas are disappearing. They'll be a part of your dated folklore, like the glaciers.

Like Grandpa said, while sipping on a warm beer on a cold day, "Everything in moderation."

Find the balance. You're in this for the long haul. And so is your kid. Choose their lessons wisely.

What Kind Of World Will They Enter?

The lessons your kid learns will give them the tools to enter the real world. A future real world we do not yet know. We can think and imagine, but who can predict what the earth and society will look like in the twenty-three years it will take to get the kid from pregnancy through college?

Will there be war? Global warming? Food shortage? Water shortage? Oil shortage? Will there be an asteroid on the way, yet to be discovered, ready to cause widespread panic as people prepare to die in a cataclysmic event?

While you ask those questions and decide on the answers, just know you're probably wrong. Wrong because there is no way to predict what will come your child's way during their day-to-day activities. Wrong because some socially awkward techie is going to partner with a group of unempathetic capitalists and create more products to isolate, distract, and thrust society closer to the dystopian future of our dreams. Wrong because the asteroid has been discovered, and it's being kept a secret to prevent chaos. That was on the Internet.

What's the solution? Build a bubble. Every day, help your child become more and more comfortable with denial. Help them ignore the problems of the world instead of engaging in them. Teach them that change and despair don't exist. Do your job, and they'll live their lives in the bubble that you help them build. A bubble that will never be popped, giving your kid the freedom to live their reality in a fantasy world.

Or you could teach them to be comfortable with change. You can teach them to develop the mental flexibility to deal with popped bubbles. You can teach them to find comfort with change and to view it as a service and not a disservice.

How Do You Make That Happen?

How do you help your child become comfortable with change?

You let them deal with challenges. You let them fail ... and fail hard. Let them go buck wild failing. Let them fail building the best block tower in the world with a single block base. Let them fail at making popcorn by topping it with cayenne pepper and sugar. Let them fail while they try to fly off the roof with a few pieces of cardboard and some string.

Teach your child that failing is okay. Teach them that learning is an ongoing process. Teach them that living life means experiencing the good *and* the bad. Let them eat your favorite chocolate bonbons. Then give them a chocolate-covered brussels sprout. Change happens when they least expect it. They'll learn that one quickly. Plus, they'll never steal Mommy's candy again.

Let your kid fail. Then help them get up off the pavement, or wash out their mouth, and try again.

Unless it's life threatening, in which case ... stop them!!

Chapter 2

Working Vs. Stay-At-Home

A debate has lingered on through the ages. This debate produces seeds of resentment. Seeds fertilized with the term *working* parent. It's a travesty, a cruel fucking joke, that the word *work* is associated with the parent who leaves for ten to twelve hours a day to associate with other adults.

What's even more of a travesty is that the caretaking parent is referred to as the nonworking parent, yet this parent seems to work more than their fair share ... and is not appreciated at all. They're looked down upon at dinner parties, which they don't make it to because childrearing never stops. But if they did actually make it to dinner parties, they'd be patronized with a bunch of bullshit like, "What do you actually do all day?"

What makes matters worse is that for decades, the parent with the job—like a high-level executive—has taken all the credit for the work of others. They've been considered the head of the household. What the fuck?! They don't do shit around the household.

Not to take away from the pains of leaving your kid every day. You *working* parents shouldn't be denied the frustration you experience when you miss out on all the memories, milestones, and accomplishments of your kid. A kid who might not even realize that you're related to them. But don't play yourselves. Your caretaking partner is a saint, if you're lucky enough to have a partner who is doing the majority of the caregiving. If you do, you should count your blessings, because it's the hardest job in the world.

Why? Because it never ends. You're always on. You're always worrying. It's taxing. Then you're forced to listen to the other parent complain about how they have to go schmooze at work functions. Or how they had a business lunch on the company's dime at the pretentious, upscale restaurant around the corner. Must be nice. Meanwhile, you get to try to convince yourself and the world that you are contributing.

While gender lines are changing, and more fathers are staying home enduring the daily shit that women, for centuries, have experienced with a convincing smile— if you believe television— let's take this opportunity to thank the caretakers of past and present and say *women are the stronger sex.* Hands down.

For centuries, women have done all of the home stuff *and* still ego stroked those *working* adults who had too many drinks on the job. *Working* adults who, instead of coming home to help, passed out in their leather chair, with a grip of death on one last drink.

To the women of the world: You're stronger.

To the stay-at-home parents of the world: You work harder.

To the "real men" of the world, who spend their free time passionately lifting heavy objects in the gym like a Neanderthal, or who go to work in suits pretending to be the greatest thing since red wine: The gig is up.

What About The Other Parent?

But, alas, the parent who leaves each day does make plenty of sacrifices of their own. They don't get much credit for missing milestones. Their kid's first step could very well be during the weekly company meeting. The first word could be during that daily, crappy commute. Then as their kid grows up, there are missed practices and games, missed homework and projects, missed movies and stories, missed or distracted vacations—all reminders of their own inadequacies as a parent. All plot holes in their story of perfect parenting.

The sacrifice of the parent who leaves each day, while different than that of the caretaker, is just as real. There is nothing worse than missing out on the moments that make or break your kid's life.

In fact, some of you are going to miss most of the milestones. Your kid won't even know who you are. You'll be the vaguely familiar person who occasionally pays for dinner. You'll be the parent who doesn't know the hobbies. You'll be the parent who won't know your kid's friends or the friends' parents. The friends' parents who actually show up for stuff. You'll never meet their teachers. You won't know what to do when the kid is sick. You won't know their food allergies or what foods to feed them. Your relationship to your family will be tied to your ability to pay for stuff, and that's the extent of it.

That's a hard road to travel down. One day, your kid will grow up and bombard you with questions about why you were not there ... ever ... for anything. You'll get defensive and try to justify it all away. You'll say things like "I was working" or "I was the provider so you could have your fabulous life!" Or you'll catch yourself thinking, "Watch your mouth, you ungrateful little shit! Who raised you?"

Deep down, you'll know the answer to that question. It was the other parent. Deep down, you'll know the kid is right. Maybe you should have worked a little less and helped out at home a little more. Or at least sat there, watching sports, while the kid was on the floor.

That dilemma is part of *your* quest, and it's your burden to carry. Be careful—the allure of gold is tempting.

RELATIONSHIP CHANGES

Regardless of your role, the relationship between you and your partner in the quest will change forever.

The innocent days of smoking a bowl, getting drunk, and frolicking through the house naked are gone. And while the frolicking naked might ultimately return, as long as the kid eventually moves out—and more importantly, you two are still together—it'll be a little different twenty-three years later.

It's important to take the state of your relationship into consideration from the beginning.

If your relationship is actually pretty fragile, or your significant other is annoying as hell, or you argue every day about important things like putting away the dishes, then maybe they're not the right person to have a child with.

A child will only make things harder.

It takes hard work to maintain a relationship. That workload is doubled when a kid is involved. Maybe even tripled. If your relationship is built around biting your tongue, grinning and bearing it, or hoping things will get better, you're fucked. Why? Because both of you are filling up a pool of resentment, and your new little addition is basically a firehose. No one wants to run around naked when you're carrying around a pool of slimy resentment water inside of you.

If that's a great description of your relationship, or you read it, and it immediately triggered denial, welcome to the club. From now on, you're like the rest of us, parenting with someone who has flaws. You're playing a winner-takes-all game of psychological warfare, where the other side knows all of your weaknesses. Prepare for the cold, lonely, sexless nights—they are headed your way, like nose blindness in a nursery. You know... the parent who smells like diapers, butt cream, and baby formula masked with perfume? That's now you.

But there is hope.

The Importance
Of Talking ... Honestly

Honesty. Practice it now. Let's try it. Think of an honest thought, open your mouth, and say it out loud.

You do it all the time. You open your mouth and talk. You talk and talk and talk about stupid shit, but you never practice talking about deep, honest shit. Why? Because, it's intimidating. Who wants to reveal their inner thoughts, vulnerabilities, and insecurities? No one. So why start now? You're about to be a parent. And parents don't talk about honest shit. They put on a happy face and live in denial for years. That's what it means to be a parent. Suck it up and fool yourself until it all crumbles.

Well, not anymore. Here you talk about honest shit. While you're prepping for that baby to come out, practice airing your grievances. You need to know it's not the end of the world when you air grievances with your partner.

Honest talk is hard, though. It takes coaching. It takes training wheels. It takes padding. Start with the easy stuff before diving into the deeper issues. Easy stuff like ...

"Your perfume makes you smell like a greasy old man."
"Your eyebrows are too bushy."
"Your cooking tastes like vomit."

Do *not* dive into the hard stuff. Hard stuff like ...

"You're mediocre in bed."
"I actually preferred your sibling over you."
"I was thinking of someone else when we conceived this child."

That is *not* the kind of honesty you need. There is a line that you need to draw, and you'll know when you've crossed it. It'll be made very clear when the pool of resentment floods, sending you to the sofa when you least expect it.

Once you have practiced honest talk, the ground work will be laid to travel on this quest together. That is, as long as you're on the same page of the book. Your partner might still be stuck questioning whether they should be a parent. In which case, good luck.

Chapter 3

YOUR ENTIRE LIFE
IS ABOUT TO CHANGE

You know that though. You know *everything* is about to change. Your life, your house, your relationship, your free time, the food you eat, how much you drink, how much you exercise, how often you see friends, how much money you have, where you travel, how you talk, what you read, how you watch movies, the way you view the world ... the list goes on and on, but why ruin the surprise?

You are about to be run over by the change bus, and there is nothing you can do about it. Either embrace it or face the consequences when your kid grows up to be an asshole.

Setting Realistic Expectations
For How Life Will Actually Be

The first step to embracing your new life of change is to set some realistic expectations of what that change looks like. Change is hard and parents lie. By now you've heard the stereotypical comments from your parent friends:

"Oh, it's great. They grow so fast. He's only one and already practically potty trained."

"The kiddo latched right on, slept through the night, and hasn't been fussy at all."

"I mean, I lose a little sleep because they eat every four hours, but other than that, we're great."

Lies. Lies. Lies.

Your friends are lying to you. They're putting you on. They're miserable but don't want to admit it. Those cheeky fucks want you to experience their pain too. Misery loves company. Misery doesn't want you to learn from its mistakes. Misery wants you to blindly run into a snake den so your friends can watch you scream.

That's not what this book is about. This book is about honesty and authenticity. Here are some real examples of what it's really like:

"I didn't sleep a wink for seven days. Every time the kid moved, I thought they needed something, and every time they were quiet, I thought they were dying."

"I automatically babbled when I tried to talk to people. It happened for weeks. I developed gray hair, crow's feet, and a bald patch on my legs. I have yet to recover."

"I only drank coffee and diet soda for three weeks. I ate cookies for five months. I was truly convinced a jar of pureed yams was gourmet."

That's how it really is. Couple that with the fact you won't leave the house for months.

Luckily, it doesn't last forever. One day, after three months in the living room, you'll decide being depressed and cooped up in the house will no longer work. It will be time to venture out into society and face your fear: the outside world. You'll shave for the first time in a month and take a shower for what could be the first time in three days—you're not quite sure. You will feed the kid. Dress the kid. Dress yourself. Pack the big diaper bag with all of the essentials. Pack the backup diaper bag with all of the essentials. Charge the phone. Charge the backup phone in case something happens to your regular phone. You'll do one last diaper check. Fuck. It'll need to be changed. You'll think, "I'm not going upstairs again. I'll change the diaper on the living room floor."

While changing the diaper, you'll hear a jogger out front. You'll watch the jogger, a seventy-five-year-old man, pass closely by and glance over at the empty stroller. You'll yell, "I've got my eye on you, criminal!" While you do that, you'll fail to notice the purple hue on your kid's face. You'll turn back just in time to witness an explosion. An explosion all over you, the carpet, the sofa, and the dog, who unsuspectingly sat beside you, lonely and desperate for attention.

You'll clean up everything—which will include your bath, the kid's bath, the dog's bath, a carpet cleaning, a sofa cleaning, a change of everyone's clothing, the next feeding, and another diaper change—and you'll be tired, but you will not be defeated. You are now ready to go.

Once outside, you'll realize the stroller is gone. And with it are both bags, your favorite coffee mug, your primary phone, and the backup phone. You'll call the police on the *backup's* backup, which you have hidden in your pocket. You'll know it was the old man jogger, who must have been eyeing the setup earlier.

The police will arrive quickly because you told them you were robbed at gun point, or so you thought. They'll take a statement and look around for clues but will be unable to find any. You cry. The old man is going to get away with it.

Then ... a stroke of luck. They look in the garage, which was closed, though you remember opening it to take the stroller out. Did that old man take the car seat too? You'll yell, "Fuck! The universe is conspiring against me!"

They'll open the garage door, and there, in all its glory, will be the entire setup. The thief must have been scared by the sirens and ran. And when he did, he decided to close the garage door to hide his tracks. Smart.

The police will look at you. You'll be embarrassed, you'll lie, and you'll tell the police this was your backup stroller. You'll half smile and say, "You always need a backup. You never know when an elderly man will rob you of your baby stroller."

Later that afternoon, after a lecture from the police about filing false reports, there will be a knock at the door. It will be the elderly man. He's back to take what he already took and returned, no doubt. You'll put the kid in a corner and build a wall of pillows as protection. You'll open the door. He'll smile and say, "I put the stroller in your garage earlier. Hope you found it. Didn't want anyone to take it. Have a good day."

He'll run off before you can say anything.

Defeated, you change back into sweatpants and decide that going to the driveway was enough action for the day.

It will be three more weeks before you attempt to leave the house again.

Welcome to parenting, where every day is like a J.R.R. Tolkien epic ... just to get out the front door. Where everything is overwhelming, and there is always so much shit to do.

There Is So Much Shit To Do

Yes, there is. Especially if being the perfect parent is still your goal. And because it *is* still your goal, you must have everything flawless.

A flawless room. A flawless room with colors that match. A flawless room where the matching colors are soothing yet stimulating—not too bright, not too dull. You don't want your kid to develop a personality disorder because you chose the wrong paint.

Also, flawless toys. A flawless room needs flawless toys or it's not a flawless room. The toys must be made of recycled plastic from certifiably green companies with studies that prove that their products promote healthy development. Your kid will not play with the same shit you did. It could ruin them ... like it ruined you.

And who could forget flawless books? A set of flawless

books to go in the flawless room and be read on the flawless baby glider. Read with the perfect, flawless baby-reading tone and pace. They will flawlessly learn. They will learn how to read and write flawlessly because of the flawless atmosphere they were raised in.

After the flawless room is put together, you must be sure everything else is in order: college funds, health insurance, the proper name, updated shots for everyone that will ever come in contact with your child, a proper stock of bottles and cleaners, and laundry detergent that is designed for babies. Wait. What good is laundry detergent when the old washer and dryer have been contaminated by other detergents? That won't cut it— those detergents aren't hypoallergenic. You'll need a new washer and dryer. Luckily the car seat you have is still good. But the car that goes with the car seat isn't. You need a new family car. It's a small price to pay for flawlessness.

Don't forget to sign up for all the classes you and your child need before and after birth.

Don't forget to play music through headphones designed for the womb.

Don't forget to talk to the baby, in ten-minute increments, every hour, unless the baby is sleeping, in which case, never wake a baby sleeping in the womb. That's a thing, right? It is now. The baby starts to dream in the womb at the sixth-month mark. You'd hate to interrupt and give it nightmares. Never wake a sleeping womb baby.

Don't forget to research schools. It will be here before you know it.

And are you exercising and eating well? You're not? There's a study on that, too. It's a good way to ensure your kid won't get a perfect SAT score.

All those thoughts, spun from the giant spider of fear. A spider you must battle on your quest. You need to battle it before it entangles you.

How do you battle a giant spider of fear? Nothing popped up on Google. Good thing you have *The Greatest Parenting Book Ever* to answer that question. You battle it with a plan. Not just any plan, though. *The* plan.

The Plan

You need a plan to prioritize all this shit. Being a perfect parent is impossible enough, but expecting it to happen without a plan of action is psychotic.

So let's make your plan.

At the top of your plan, write the following: Perfection is the breeding ground of misery.

Below that, write:

> Figure out which room is available.
> Clean the room.
> Get furniture for the room.
> Put furniture in the room.
> Decide between nursing and formula.
> Buy the basics: clothing, rags, bottles, diapers, wipes.
> Wash what you need to.

That was easy. The plan is done.

Now that you have the baby necessities out of the way, you can plug away at whatever else you *want* to. But you've done everything you *have* to.

If your kid grows up mad that their room wasn't a specific shade of green, then you have a much larger problem on your hands. Well-adjusted adults don't tend to whine about their nursery room decorations, or lack thereof.

By the way, your child can't even see clearly until month three, so you have a few extra months to get your flawlessness together ... if you must.

Take the pressure off. It'll all be okay.

Chapter 4

THE BABY INDUSTRY: MARKETING TO FEAR

Like all industries, the Baby Industry doesn't want to solve your problems. They would rather give you fast-acting, temporary relief. Like an antacid company that encourages customers to eat what they want, when they want, with the promise to save you from the gluttony ... the Baby Industry does the same.

The Baby Industry strings you along, providing nothing more than temporary light during your quest through the impermeable darkness of parenting. They promise that you're only a few dollars shy and a little time away from finally achieving the perfect family you've been longing for. They frame every problem with high stakes and high pressure. You're in the world series, bottom of the ninth, and you're about to lose the game for the team. They are the relief pitcher who has come to save the game—and your life—from crumbling away.

The Industry holds a carrot that you'll never catch. They don't care about you. They care about their stakeholders. They don't want you to know that the majority of the shit they sell won't make a difference in your kid's life. Hell, most of the stuff you'll buy won't get used for more than a day. The Industry is full of manipulative masters who exploit your FOFUYCL. You know why that baby in the commercial is so happy and bouncy and clapping? They're celebrating. Celebrating that Mommy and Daddy are being fucked over.

The Industry knows that you want the perfect family. They also know when you see that smiling baby and happy family—they've got you. You give them your trust. And when you trust them, you'll trust the product being sold. You'll think, "If I follow their little, shiny light in a sea of darkness, I will succeed in my quest to have that perfect family."

Unfortunately, you won't see their razor-sharp teeth until it's too late.

The thing with the Industry is this: It attacks from multiple sides. If, somehow, you don't get caught up in the FOFUYCL, then you'll get caught on the flip side with the shame from the parenting community.

The Shame

The shame is the worst. Marketers know if you don't get caught up in the initial fear, you'll get caught when the parenting community breaks you with their wrath. You awful human being.

Shame sounds like this:

"Are you really going to let your kid do that?"

"What is she wearing? She can't be seen like that."

"How could you deprive your child of a happy life? Haven't you seen the studies?"

Need to hear more?

You can always count on the parenting community to make you feel like an epic failure. For instance, you'll encounter a brisk, fifty-five-degree day. You'll bundle up your child with an extra blanket. Your child will make it apparent that the extra blanket is too hot by throwing it on the ground. After tucking your child in fifteen times, you'll finally give up and put the blanket in the bag. Your child will go from fussy to happy. Your child will start blowing bubbles and drooling and making indistinguishable sounds of happiness, but like clockwork, you'll notice that the happier your baby is, the more scowls other adults will direct toward you.

You'll think, "Did something happen in the world today that I don't know about?"

Then it'll hit you. Some overly friendly, smiling asshole will approach you. You'll immediately wonder if they are going to ask for money or try to get touchy and pinch the kid's cheeks.

Then, just as quickly, they'll say something like, "Doesn't Daddy or Mommy have a blanket for you?"

You'll answer right back, "Of course, it's right here. She was hot." You'll pull out the blanket from the bag.

Then the stranger, who isn't so nice to you anymore, will snatch the blanket out of your hand and try to tuck in your child. They'll say, "Your Daddy or Mommy really should have you tucked in." The tone is half baby talk, half smug sarcasm.

You'll try to defend yourself, but ultimately, no matter what you say, there is no excuse for this level of neglect. Then, once the baby is tucked in, a look of disgust will again fall upon the face of the not-so-nice stranger. They'll glare at you and say, "You really should have a clean blanket."

They'll storm off, pointing and glaring back at you with anyone they come across, never giving you the opportunity to explain that the *baby* threw the blanket on the ground.

Oh ... blame it on your kid. Typical.

Traumatized, you'll rush home, cry in a corner, order a blanket that can be attached to the stroller, overnight it so your baby doesn't have to suffer any longer, and never return to that place again.

That's shame. All parents are afraid of shame. It's time to bid it adieu.

Trendy Parenting

There will always be new issues to be afraid of and new bandwagons to join. Those bandwagons come with a new wave of shame and fear to fend off.

Parenting trends are perfectly timed storms that bring total destruction mere weeks after recovering from previous storms. Parenting trends are a sleeping dragon. A sleeping dragon that awakens to breathe fire on everything you've spent months or even years to build.

Parenting trends come and go as quickly as a media cycle, which is why you should pay no attention to them, like brats at a birthday party. Anything worth incorporating into your child's life needs long-term proof. What good is a one-year study if it fails to identify that at year five, the majority of children become serial killers?

A study full of five-year-old serial killers ... that's a career ender.

Trendy parenting exploits words like *statistics* or *majority*. Trendy parenting knows that you don't remember shit from math class. A majority is anything over half. You can have a majority and still practically have a one in two chance that your kid won't be a serial killer.

Congratulations.

The worst parenting trends make you feel they have withstood the test of time, though they haven't. They tell you their ideas are what your dear, sweet, innocent grandmother would want. They tell you that their ideas helped your grandmother and grandfather be successful parents. They tell you that it wasn't until your parents moved away from your dear grandmother and grandfather that they were ruined by society.

Your parents were not ruined by society. They were ruined by something else. TV families. And who put your ruined parents in front of the TV? Dear, sweet, innocent grandmother and grandfather.

Your parents were part of the first generation caught and brainwashed by the allure of the TV family. Your parents developed a bitterness toward their parents because they could see, every night, the extent of their deprived childhoods. They developed a bitterness that caused them to throw away the time-tested parenting methods that worked for their non-TV watching ancestors. A bitterness resulting in trendy parenting. A culture of abrupt judgments, exaggerated reactions, and short-term solutions.

Blame it all on grandmother and grandfather.

Trendy parenting will never get you closer to your goals. Like your parents' goals, your goals don't exist. Like the TV family, perfect parenting is fiction. You have become your parents. You fell for the Internet like they fell for the TV. Luckily, everything on the Internet is real.

Old-School Tips

Since new-school parenting is all about keeping up with trends that exist in a fictional world, your quest is to take things back to the basics. Your quest is to pursue reality. Old-school reality. And once you find it, share it with the world.

The quest is tough. There will be obstacles. You'll be a magical ninja in training, facing your fear. You'll be Hermione helping Harry Potter by using the spell of reality to shed light on the truth. You'll be a unicorn, like Pegasus (who wasn't a unicorn), and you'll come down from the heavens to help save your fellow parents of the world.

Except those are all stories. Fuck—reality is hard.

Luckily, Grandpa has given quite a few pieces of advice over the years. Advice worth sharing.

Grandpa's old-school tips:

*   *Child* is synonymous with *inconvenient.* Get used to it.
*   Babies cry. Get used to it.
*   Your favorite china will break. Get used to it.
*   Parenting is nothing like TV. Get used to it.
*   When you think you have parenting mastered, the other shoe drops and fucks it all up. Get used to it.
*   Don't fall for FOMO: fear of missing out.
*   Have a healthy amount of FOGRO: fear of getting ripped off. Snake oil is bountiful and looks like the real thing, but like a knock-off bag from Chinatown, it breaks down and crumbles as soon as you start using it. Be on the lookout.

Chapter 5

BABY SHOWERS ...
TO WASH THEMSELVES CLEAN

You've made it. The baby shower, where other people celebrate you with food, drinks, gifts, and awful games. Nothing, absolutely nothing, will ever make the games fun. Yet you grin and say, "Thank you!" After all, it's all about you. You appreciate that. You love that in fact, because you're starting to have doubts about being a parent.

You're starting to get a little scared. You're getting close to the delivery date, and you just don't know how you're going to make it through. Then, with a timing pulled straight from your dreams, your friends and family swoop in with all the love, support, and good vibrations of the world. They swoop in to reassure you that it will all be okay. They remind you that it takes a village.

The day of the baby shower is a brilliant day. Your friends and family shower you with *gifts*. Gifts that will *help*. Gifts that will help *them* alleviate their guilt when they disappear. The baby shower is a ritualistic cleansing of guilt that they prepared for themselves. They wash themselves clean of the obligation to help and leave you for dead with a smile, a hug, and an artificial-grass drying rack.

Think about that in your time of need.

When you're in the middle of the war on laundry, no one will be around. Why? Because they got you a bag to wash the stuffed animals in.

When you're in the middle of the war on dishes, no one will be around. Why? Because they got you an organic kitchen sponge shaped like your crying baby.

When you're in the middle of the war on sleep, no one will be around. Why? Because they got you a sheepskin, vibrating mattress pad. Baa.

It takes a village, and your village left you with a bunch of shit. And then they ghosted you.

It Takes A Village ...
Where The Fuck Are They?

Yep, like clockwork. They'll ghost you. Oh, they'll see the baby once or twice in the first week or two. But after that, the phrase you'll hear the most is, "It's been forever, where have you been?"

You'll think, "At home, raising a child. Where the fuck have you been?"

It takes a village, but it's not the village you thought it would be.

Here's a piece of advice: Entrap those soon-to-be flakes. Tell them you want time and help, not baby shower gifts. You don't need their bullshit bag of nipple protectors and rash creams.

Tell them to bring their rumps over to help with laundry and to get the vomit off of your favorite, frumpy sweatshirt.

Tell them you want someone to come over and make a week's worth of prepackaged dinners so you can break the cookie and diet soda habit before it even starts.

Tell them you want a babysitter who is worth a damn and a shoulder to cry on. If they can't handle that, tell them to pool their money and pay for therapy and a babysitter so you can cry on someone else's shoulder!

What *You* Need And How To Ask For It

This is the time to figure out what you need and to ask for it. Maybe that includes some of the suggestions from above. Maybe not. Whichever the case, you need to keep your expectations real and not live in the fantasy world you've created. If you stay in your fantasy world, you'll pretend everything is all right. You'll pretend that this too shall pass. You'll fool yourself. You'll give people the benefit of the doubt, and you won't get the help you *need*.

Ask for help! If your friends and family get hurt because you asked for help with dinner, then you have shitty friends and family. Better to find that out now instead of waiting, full of hopes and delusions, for the day that everyone can read your mind and figure out that you're struggling.

On the other hand, friends *should* know what you need. Being an overwhelmed parent in need of help with basic life activities isn't a new concept. They probably went through it themselves. Unless, of course, you're the first parent in your social group, in which case, whip those motherfuckers into shape.

If you're not the first parent, the reason you're not getting help is simple. Misery loves company. Misery doesn't want you to learn from your friends' mistakes.

Real playground talk: Plan for your village to leave your ass in the dust unless you speak up. No one is going to help you until you ask for their help. Point blank. That's the next skill to master on your quest. How to ask, "This is what I need—can you do it?"

It's your team; be the leader. Run point guard. Play quarterback. Stand there and chew gum like a true shortstop. It's your world; quack like a duck and run it.

THE DIRTY SECRET OF PARENTING

Ready for the dirty secret of parenting?

Parents are the most spiteful, rancorous liars in the world. They're all smiles, nods, and ... backstabbing liars. It runs deep.

When parents see other parents struggling with a child throwing a tantrum ... they smile. They smile and think, "Glad it's not me."

When parents hear about the naive hopes and dreams of soon-to-be parents, they think, "Let me know how that works out ... idiots."

When parents hear new parents speak honestly about what's really going on, they shame the new parents into silence. Why? Because raising a child is incredibly difficult, and they bask in watching new parents struggle. Fooling new parents for the fun of it is a rite of passage. Seasoned parents made it through their shit; now it's time for the new parents to suffer.

Besides, those new parents were the ones saying, "How hard could it be?"

Those new parents were saying things like, "It's not like you work. What do you do all day?"

Those new parents were also saying, "I have my degree. It's not that hard. I'll be fine."

The dirty secret of parenting: Parents can't wait to watch you experience the hell they went through. Every complaint or struggle from new parents brings a moment of joy to established parents.

A Culture of
Isolation And Secrecy

Isolation and secrecy—a few weeks in, and those two topics will be on your mind. You'll find yourself thinking, "I'm so alone. Why didn't anybody warn me about this?"

Now you know why: because other parents want to know you're struggling for their own entertainment.

Parents will isolate you to break you down like baby food. They'll do that to see if you're worthy. To see if you can pass the test.

It's part of the initiation process. When someone finally makes contact with you, you'll be excited. You'll be pumped. You'll rise out of the ashes of isolation with your stroller, a new person. You'll potentially be social again.

Parents break you down first because they don't want honest socialization—it's a reminder of the misery of their own lives. You can never be truly honest in your new social group. No one wants to actually hear about your struggles—they just want to see the hints. You'll learn to fake it till you make it. It's all a big sham, where you smile and say, "Oh, it's been a breeze."

If you don't play along, you'll be isolated from your new group.

Parenting is a club of secrecy, and you can never spill its secrets. If you do, you'll be thrown out by your peers, right back to the beginning stage: isolation. You'll be tasked with the burden of going through the process again. Do you want that? Of course you don't.

The first rule of parenting? Don't talk honestly about parenting.

Building Your Village ... Playground-Mafia Style

Everyone knows it's a sham, but you'll play the game. You'll join the group. You'll help bring on new members. You'll do your due diligence to make sure they don't kill the illusion. Then one day, you'll look around and realize you've built a village. A village of cold-hearted, battle-tested parents who know what's up, yet they don't talk honestly. A village where everyone sits around on their thrones of perfectly folded laundry to gossip about those that haven't yet earned their place at the table. Your new village will have conversations based on bullshit about how easy it is. Delusional fucks. Parents are liars.

Then, one magical day, someone will be a little too tired and will drop the honesty bomb, blowing all pretense out of the water. Magically, that person will be handed the squeaky hammer of judgment and become the leader. The leader of a real Playground Mafia. That leader will be you. You will decide when it's time to reach out to a new struggling parent, after harshly criticizing their mistakes and shortcomings. You'll invite them for a test drive and judge them by whether they brought you coffee.

One by one, your village built on honesty will grow. A sense of humor will rise out of the communal misery, and you will have built your very own Playground Mafia. All because you dropped the honesty bomb. Boom.

That day is yours to seize. Seize the day. Drop the honesty bomb.

SURVIVING PREGNANCY

But to get to that day, you must emotionally survive pregnancy. And pregnancy is psychological warfare for everyone. Right now, you don't give a fuck about anything, which proves the point that you're pregnant. You're creating a life inside of you. You're creating the first ~~dictator emperor supreme~~ leader of the world, and the world needs to respect that.

Yet, while you love having the world bow at your every need, you are *over it*. You're forty weeks in and *done*. You're ready to get back to normalcy, which you can barely remember. You're tired of carrying around the extra weight. And sweating. And wearing flip-flops in the middle of winter. Your taste buds are so messed up, you don't even know what to eat. And you're moody ... damn, are you moody. You cry during Dave Chappelle and feel like your people are from *Orange is the New Black* because the orange suits remind you of pumpkins, which is what you feel like in your current state. You are trapped in the prison of pregnancy.

But there is hope. You're almost there. You're just a few short days or weeks away from the best drugs you will have in your life. Endorphins and oxytocin will flood your brain. Then you'll return home with a new addition to the family. You'll return to normal. You have all the baby necessities, and your friends and family will be there for you, without even asking.

You're almost there. Normal. Picture it. Normal, with a slight inconvenience. You are days away from the best sleep of your life. Let that be your inspiration to push ahead.

Chapter 6

It Is So Much Harder
Than You Ever Imagined

You made it. Pat yourself on the back, if you can reach it.
You made it through pregnancy. It's time to get back to a
normal life.

Except you have a child now. Pregnancy was the easy stuff.
This is your new normal, and your new normal sucks. It
is so much harder than you ever imagined, because you
can't imagine. You literally can't imagine what it is like to
be *on* twenty-four hours a day, three hundred sixty-five
days a year, with your child always on your mind. You're
always worrying ... somewhere, deep down. It's like there
is a part of your brain whose only job is to subconsciously
worry about your child.

When you imagined what it would be like as a parent, there was so much you didn't consider. That's normal. It's a part of the process. Everyone goes through that. Everyone says, "Why the fuck didn't anyone warn us about this?"

But here's the thing—you *were* warned. You can go back to the early chapters of this book and see that there was plenty of warning, but you refused to listen. You were still trying to create the perfect family. You were still trying to be a perfect parent. You were still in denial.

Remember when you thought, "How hard could it be? I have my degree." How is your degree helping you right about now? Did it prepare you for constantly being needed? You're probably in need of a break right now. Is your partner back to work? You're probably already building resentment toward your partner, who gets a break every day.

You were warned. You didn't listen.

... AND IT DOESN'T STOP

No, it doesn't. You're about to get well acquainted with what's on television at three thirty in the morning. Reruns of TV shows with perfect families and infomercials for products aimed at helping you in your need.

That's the Industry: there to tempt you with a fantasy and follow it with a quick fix.

It's incredible how dreary and bleak the world becomes when you haven't slept for a few days. You'll start lying, like a typical parent. You'll tell people, "It's fine. I get an hour here and thirty minutes there. I'm good."

No you're not. You're lying to yourself.

This is the point in your quest where you need to fall back on your training. You need to ask for what you want. Pick up the phone in your desperate time of need and call in the village. An hour of sleep here and a half hour there isn't enough. You need help. More help than you're getting. ASK FOR IT.

Or maybe you should consider hiring help ...

SHOULD YOU HIRE HELP?

Oh, and your ego will take a blow. After all, it's *your* child, and you were going to stay home to raise them. You had it all planned out. You mapped it out perfectly. Notice a trend? It never goes as planned.

It's a hard pill to swallow when you consider hiring help. Not everyone does. Not everyone can. But there is no shame for those that do. There is no award for the most rundown parent. There is no award for the parent who suffered the most. Fuck that. Besides, you could have someone helping you eight hours a day and still work harder than you have in your entire life. Parenting is that hard.

In the olden days, people had parents, aunts, uncles, jesters, wet nurses, nanny dogs, and their much younger siblings to help raise their child. Not anymore. You took off on your own across the country. There is no family within a two thousand-mile radius. Deal with your ego and put in a call. A couple of hours a day or a couple of nights a week can easily be the difference between being a hypersensitive zombie or just being a zombie ... or just sensitive.

The sooner you ask for help, the better.

The Myth Of Who Comes First

There is a common notion that when you become a parent, your child automatically becomes number one. The first priority. Numero uno. While aspects of that principle are spot on, there's a problem that needs to be addressed.

Obviously, when you are born into this sick, cruel, dark world, with blurry vision and no muscle tone, you must depend on the kindness of others. Just as obvious, if you opt for a drunken night where you and your sweet lover make the decision that it's time to unnecessarily complicate your life and relationship by having a child, then it's your responsibility to take care of that dependent, little blob and grow it into some semblance of a person. Thus, because the blob's life is dependent on the kindness of others, and you had a drunken frolic, it comes first.

But you can't let the little leech kill you. You can't let the kid chop you down and leave nothing but a stump to sit on, taking away your ability to provide oxygen and fruit. You could teach them to make bricks and reap the benefits of a home that won't be destroyed by termites. A home of bricks next to a tree, still intact, that provides the life blood of all humanity.

You don't teach that, though. You choose to teach your child that positive parenting is about giving so much of yourself that you die ... because working yourself to death is so healthy.

Bringing Your A Game

If you love your family, you should want to give them your A game, right? You don't want to drain yourself so much that you grace them with the opportunity to experience your D game. Who wants that?

There are resources that provide help and relief. Seek them out. Use them. Just because your kid comes first doesn't mean everything needs to come from you!

Take care of number one so you can take care of your number one.

Taking Care of Number One

Taking care of number one—so that you can take care of your number one—can take some imagination. Imagination that you have been developing for months while you prepped for the fantasy world you imagined parenting to be.

Maybe you don't have a lot of money. Maybe you feel isolated. Maybe you're too busy throwing yourself a pity party to think of something that will actually help you feel better. Whatever the excuse, it's time to get proactive. Get creative. Take responsibility for giving yourself a break.

Once you get that break and start to recharge, you'll notice that the weight of the world lifts ever so slightly from your shoulders. When that happens, you'll feel something that you have been longing for: relief. A brief moment of relief. When you get that relief, you start to recharge. Then you'll be able to give something that is much closer to your A game, and your family will thank you for it one day ... maybe.

It takes work to get a break, and the break might only be little moments here and there, but that's how the cookie crumbles for superheroes. You're expected to save the world at a moment's notice. And that's a problem, because you're not a superhero.

The Problem With Superheroes

The problem with superheroes is they're fiction. They don't exist. They're not real.
You knew that, right? Yet you put expectations on yourself that would make it seem like you're nothing short of superhuman.

The other problem with superheroes is that they don't know when or how to say no. They can't. They're trapped. Trapped by the helpless victims of a society who need them. Trapped by their own superhero guilt. Trapped because ... what kind of superhero has doubts and needs help?

We love superheroes. We love that a superhero has a tremendous amount of pressure placed on them, and in the end, they ultimately manage. But you're not a superhero. You're a *real* person. Maybe you should act like one.

Get some help. Take a break. Relieve yourself of the pressure to save your kid from everything. Take off the pressure to be a superhero. You don't need to be one. You need to be a parent.

When the kid falls and scrapes a knee, stand there, watch, and say, "Are you okay?" Then calmly pick them up and put a bandage on their owie. You can do that without freaking out. Shit happens. At some point, kids need to learn how to deal with life, without being saved. Learning the hard way is sometimes the best way.

Once you drop the superhero act, the funniest thing will happen. Your kid will learn they can handle life on their own. They'll also learn they have someone to help them up when they need it. They'll have a real hero instead of a fictional comic book character. That real hero is you.

Taking Care Of Yourself Vs. Being A Selfish Fuck

There's a difference. A big difference. If you don't know the difference, your kids are doomed. It's hard, though, to admit it to yourself. All parents are liars—you know this—including you, and you'll find that you lie to yourself all the time. You'll find that you tell yourself you're taking care of number one, when really, you're being a selfish fuck.

You're being a selfish fuck when you go out for the fourth

night in a row to get trashed with your single, childless friends from college. You'll adamantly tell everyone there that you *need* that time to fully recharge. Meanwhile, your kid is at home crying because they haven't seen you all week.

You're being a selfish fuck when you tell your kids you're too sick to play, knowing damn well you're just hungover because you went ape shit with the cosmos and ended up at some raunchy strip club at two in the morning eating hot wings.

You're being a selfish fuck when, the day before school starts, you shop for yourself and ultimately run out of time to get the necessary school supplies for the kid. But your new outfit looks good, right?

Taking care of yourself is different. Taking care of yourself is hiring a babysitter for two hours to get a massage because the past two weeks have been hell.

Taking care of yourself is having the kid learn how to nap in the stroller so you can meet friends for coffee every other week or so.

Taking care of yourself is finding a hobby that is compatible with your new life. A hobby that helps you feel productive and engaged on a different level than you do with baby toys.

See the difference?

Baby-Centric Or No?

No ... and yes.

Of course, your child's needs come first while you take care of yourself, but your child does not—let's repeat that—does *not* get to dominate every aspect of life. Your baby needs to mold to *your* life. Not the other way around.

It's pretty simple. If the kid learns that a little crying, whining, or even sweet talk will get them out of something you have planned, then they have successfully figured out how to run your household. They will be in charge. Not you. You run shit here. The kid can nap in the stroller. The kid can eat lunch at the park. The kid can look at a picture book and color at the restaurant.

But that doesn't mean you get to be a selfish fuck. There's balance with this. Take care of yourself ... while putting the kid first. That means most of the time you're sticking to some sense of a routine. But you don't have to fall into a full-on panic if something occasionally changes. Let them learn how to deal with a little change. It builds character. It's not just about you, and it's not just about your kid.

It's About Your Kid *And* You ... Not Just Your Kid

If you're lucky, the relationship between you and your child will be a relationship that will last the rest of your life. So it's probably a good idea to become familiar with one of the most common, three-letter "A" words in the English language:

And.

What three letter word were you thinking about?

And. It's about you *and* your child. Any parent-child balance without the word *and* is suspect. If you teeter too far one way, you'll raise a needy, clingy, perpetual victim of society. A prime target that the growing industry of mental health professionals can profit from. If you teeter too far the other way, you'll raise a selfish, entitled, bratty fuck. I'm sure we all know one or two of those.

And opens up life to more possibilities. *And* opens your life to connecting with others. *And* helps you take care of yourself and your family. *And* keeps you vibrant and alive. *And* helps you take chances and solve problems. *And.* Everyone wins.

That's the power of *and*. The greatest three letter "A" word in the English language since the other greatest three letter "A" word: *ask*. Oh, were you thinking about the three letter "A" word that got you into this mess in the first place? No, you have a kid now—you won't get any of that for a while.

Chapter 7

An Array Of Emotions

This is the part in the quest where you think you're going to an amusement park but realize it's haunted. A haunted amusement park with evil clown-dogs.

The first year of your kid's life might be the scariest rollercoaster you have ever been on. Crazy scary, like that time your best friend hid in the pantry for an hour during a party, then jumped out, scared you, and caused you to crash through the kitchen table. Then everyone laughed. And so did you. You laughed hysterically before you started crying because that was your grandmother's table, and she's gone, and all that's left of her now are shattered pieces of splintered memories on the floor.

Parenting is like that. Every day. The emotional journey of a typical morning in parenting is only matched by a Shakespearean play—gibberish, with lots of yelling and crying. And that's just you. We're not even talking about your kid. Your child can run the gauntlet of emotions over the course of a minute. It's a master class.

You have to prepare yourself to live and let go. Learn to get over it. If you can't get over the crying from an hour ago, how are you going to enjoy the laughs and cuddles that are about to happen? Laughs and cuddles you just ruined because you are holding a grudge. You won't. You won't enjoy them. You'll miss them all, and you'll become a bitter, lonely hermit—frozen from a life of icing everyone out.

Save the icing for the cupcakes.

Rollercoasters go up and down. Haunted mazes have endings that you'll get to ... sometimes. Sometimes you push past the guy with a chain saw and the clown-dogs and go out the emergency exit, flipping on the lights along the way.

Parenting has an array of emotions. Dwelling on them will only keep you from moving on to the next step.

You And Your Child
Are The Same Age

Yes. You are a wobbly, babbling baby. Your age as a parent is always tied to the age of your first child. You two are the same. You have the same birthday. Your child just hit the one-month-old milestone? Congratulations, you too are only one month old.

Think about that the next time you demand the world of yourself. You're just a drooling infant, unable to distinguish shapes, and only aware of the world as a painful place where you get lots of shots, have your cheeks pinched by strangers, and have things shoved in your mouth. That's your world as a parent.

Dwell on that for a second. It's profound.

The Day-To-Day

Day-to-day life can be tough at first. Joking aside, a regular schedule of spotty sleep can make anyone feel like a crazy, windup monkey with cymbals. When you feel like that, everything sounds like it'll make your head explode.

The day-to-day struggle adds up. You develop cracks in your hands from washing them after you change a thousand diapers a day. You smell like a mixture of rice cereal, vomit, and breast milk. You spend half the day trying to figure out if your baby has a dirty diaper, or if the smell is just trapped in your nose. You thought you had the bath water temperature down, except now your baby is screaming bloody murder and you feel like the worst person in the history of the world. To top it all off, you fall asleep with the baby on your chest while trying to heat up some food in the oven for dinner, and you wake up to the smoke detector, a kitchen full of smoke, and your baby stuck between the cushions of the sofa.

This is the day-to-day crap you have to deal with on your quest. You're the ghost of Jacob Marley, and these are your chains. You've got to get out of them. Listen to some Freddy Mercury and break free. Or at least learn to live with the chains. Organize them a little. It'll make things more manageable.

How? How do you organize the chains of parenting that hold you back? By setting up a routine.

SETTING UP A ROUTINE

Nothing. Nothing beats a good routine.

Actually, that's a lie. Plenty of things are better than a good routine. Cheese is better than a good routine. Late-night pizza is better than a good routine. A bottle of your favorite beverage and an HGTV binge is better than a good routine.

But you don't have time for those shenanigans. They will distract you on your quest. Right now, you're in need of a little organization.

The most important concepts of a great routine are: where and when. The *where* isn't always important. Changing a diaper in the back of a car is always a viable option, unless that car seat is covered with cocaine, in which case, find somewhere else ... or a vacuum. But in terms of food and sleep, the most important part—other than food that is age appropriate—is the *when*.

Feeding times shouldn't be deviated from too much. Feeding doesn't have to be done in the same chair every single day. But it should be a similar time, or else you're going to see the definition of hangry.

Sleep is the same. Two o'clock might be naptime, but it can be in the stroller while you're walking or in the car while you're driving. Location changes every day might not be the most highly recommended thing to do, but every once in a while won't hurt. Warm beer on a cold day ... everything in moderation.

As you focus on what your routine with your child will be, don't forget that it should include a little time for yourself. It's not just about the kid. Maybe it's an outdoor exercise class during naptime with other parents. Maybe it's investing in a jogging stroller and actually using it. Maybe it's taking a hot bath during the kid's afternoon nap. Maybe it's just a massage once or twice a month while the babysitter is on duty. Regardless, it's your responsibility to schedule time for yourself. You need to recharge too.

Chapter 8

Relationship Maintenance

Now is about the time, while you read this book, that the first bit of relationship maintenance advice has been forgotten. It's also about the time when you realize your marriage, or partnership, or whatever you call it, is about to fall apart. One could say your relationship is a container of gasoline on a hot summer's day without the vent open, and it's about to explode.

Relationship maintenance isn't a one-off effort; it's ongoing. It's like home ownership—if you don't keep up with the little things, like checking for gas leaks, one day you'll flip on the light, and boom! you can say goodbye to more than your eyebrows.

Blowing up your relationship is not the goal ... yet. The goal is to rekindle enough of the romance that you two decide—during one tipsy night while the kid is with the grandparents—that you want to have another one.

But you're not there right now. You're not even close. Sometimes you two are just not on the same page. Sometimes you are being honest and open, and your partner is being the shittiest version of themselves possible. Sometimes your partner has job issues, or health issues, or just issues, and those issues bring about a whole slew of complications to your open, honest relationship.

Other times, it's you. You'll revert to your selfish, bratty, childless self. You'll drop the honesty and lie to keep the peace, justifying it by saying you're protecting the other person. You'll convince yourself that not being honest is the solution. And resentment starts to build. And when resentment starts to build, small annoyances suddenly become monsters in the closet.

HARBORING RESENTMENT

It starts with small grievances held inside. Little annoyances build up over time and are allowed to fester, and grow, and boil over, and explode all over everyone's face. Annoyances turn into divorceable offences. Pictures and videos of trivial milestones turn into an enormous fear of missing out. Messages about how much fun you're having in the other's absence trigger a plethora of feelings, including guilt and shame. The guilt and shame trigger the feeling of being an awful parent. The feeling of being an awful parent then triggers frustration. That frustration is redirected as anger ... at you.

You won't hear about the anger. You won't have any idea. Instead of talking about what's going on, it's stuffed. It's not discussed. Then that stuffed anger creates a divide. You sleep a little farther away from each other at night. You notice something feels off. Then that distance snowballs and becomes an avalanche. An avalanche that could have been stopped with a little harmless acting.

Remember: It's not a lie; it's acting. There is a difference. Lies cover your own ass. Acting is inclusive. Let the kid walk for a week and don't mention it at all. They won't be that good at it.

Then one day when your partner is home, act. Let the other parent see your kid walk and freak out that they saw the first step. It wasn't just one step; it was seven. They'll be so proud, and those seven steps will add to the legend of your child. Your partner will go into the office and brag that their child took seven steps on their first attempt. They'll say, "Fuck you, George in legal. My kid is the next Usain Bolt."

That's the power of acting. You can use it to let your partner think they were there for all the firsts. Why do they need to know any different? You already won. Save your-self an argument.

At the very least, don't send them videos of all the missed milestones. Send them videos of the tantrums and awful shit. Then, not only will they feel better about what they are missing, they will appreciate you more. Let them think the fun that happens throughout the day only happens when they get home. Why add to the pool of resentment?

Remember: Lies cover your own ass. Acting is inclusive.

FRIENDLY COMPETITION: A ONE-WAY TICKET TO STRIFE

Resentment is everywhere. *Everywhere.* When you're parenting with someone else, anything can turn into a bitter, all-out, emotional and psychological war.

One surefire way to start that war is with friendly competition.

"Who does that?" That's what you're thinking, right? You're thinking, "Parenting isn't a competition. It's a lov-ing quest that we are on together. We would never com-pete over our child. We don't do that."

That's good. You're well on your way to being a parent.

Your lies are getting better.

But that hippy-dippy, all-love bullshit is off the mark. Competition will happen. You will compete. One of you will say, "I wonder what the first word will be ... " And boom! Whether you realize it or not, you're both secretly hoping you'll win. Fuck the other parent. That kid is gonna say your name first.

The competition between *Mama* and *Dada* could be described as a dream killer because it has the power to destroy your dream of the perfect family. A prime example is if the kid is confused and calls Dada, *Mama* ... or Mama, *Dada*. Then you're fucked. Not only did you win, but you also stole the other parent's rightful title. Can you say, *divorce*?

The crazy part of friendly competition? Even as you sign your custody agreement, you'll be happy because deep down you'll know, forever and always, that you won.

And that's worth the divorce.

FAMILY CONTRIBUTIONS: KNOWING YOUR WORTH

The other major cause of resentment is money. Money is a hard topic for even the childless to discuss. Once you've made the decision to join accounts and potentially drop to one income—if that's even possible—you'll notice that the money conversation becomes even harder.

Once you've experienced a few weeks of consistent caregiving, you'll realize parenting is the hardest work you've ever done in your life. Yet, you'll never feel less appreciated. You'll feel invisible.

You'll feel invisible because the world, including your partner, doesn't view caretaking as an equal contribution. They don't think your stay-at-home life is equal to their work life. You'll find yourself repeating the mantra "*I* am equal" over and over, but when you're worn down and running on fumes, it becomes harder and harder to believe.

Don't be bullied into feeling like your contribution isn't equal or that you have it easy. That's a ridiculous myth. Don't fall for that shit.

A Vanilla Latte A Day

There are going to be days—hell, months—when you and your partner are running on fumes. You try to take care of yourself, but the fact still remains: Babies are hard work. One tired day, you'll put on athletic pants and a jacket, you'll put a coat over the kid's pj's, and you'll head to the local coffee shop for a vanilla latte. And it will help.

It will help you make it through the day and give you the extra kick you need to rally for the evening.

But then the habit starts. You try to skip the latte the following day, but you notice a difference. A few days go by, and all of a sudden, you're too tired to function again, so you return and order a large. And it helps. But you're DOA that night and decide you're going to drop the one-day-a-week spinning class you signed up for but don't have the energy to make it to. As the weeks pass, the lethargy creeps in. In response, you add an extra shot in what is now the first of two large vanilla lattes a day.

Slowly, over the next few months, the baggy-eyed, miserable person who looks back at you in the mirror becomes unrecognizable. You feel awful, but you can't stop. The vanilla lattes are the only thing that keep you functioning during the day because you can't sleep at night. And that's a problem. A problem with a solution: three vanilla lattes a day.

Before you know it, you have a six hundred-dollar monthly habit. You feel horrible. You step on the scale one day and realize you've gained the vanilla-latte-a-day forty. Forty pounds of vanilla latte all over your body. And you feel awful.

Let's be clear though: the problem isn't your weight. The problem is that you feel awful. You don't feel vibrant and healthy. The vanilla-latte-a-day forty is a speed bump on your quest. A blow in your self-confidence. It's a hypnotizing snake, slowly wrapping its coils around you to crush you.

SELF-CONFIDENCE

And that's why you must be diligent in your efforts to take care of yourself. When the self-confidence is gone, you'll watch a lot of other things go out the window with it ... like your favorite outfit, sex, and good times in general. But you are not alone—your partner feels awful and out of shape as well. They just don't let on. They have other adults to talk to, so they don't fester and stew during the day like you do.

Take care of yourself. You're doing a great job.

Also, coffee and tea work well for a boost. Drop the lattes.

Chapter 9

Venturing Out Into The World

It's not easy setting up a routine, but once you do, you hold on to it like a child holds on to their favorite baby blanket. But there's a problem. The routine that led you out of the house quickly becomes repetitive and mundane. Every day is the same repetitive shit. You'll go to the same playground and have the same conversation with the same people. You'll go to the same coffee shop and order the same skinny vanilla latte before you stroll the same route. You'll go to the same class, at the same outdoor staircase, holding the same skinny latte, wearing the same workout gear that you wore the same time last week. Your life becomes mundane. A repetitive, mundane day, filled with all the same mundaneness you did yesterday.

It's all the same repetitive shit. Your life becomes mundane. A repetitive, mundane day, filled with all the same mundaneness you did yesterday. It's all the same.

It's all the same repetitive shit. Your life becomes mundane. A repetitive, mundane day, filled with ... Was that already said?

Venturing out into the world is a must, but you also need to try new things, or at the very least, walk a different way home. Something, *anything* different from the prior day.

It's scary though. New places with a baby are scary. There are so many unknowns. Germs and obstacles, and assholes who bump into you while you're waiting in line, and mentally disturbed drug addicts who make you stand on the bus while holding two bags and a child.

And what do you take to a new place? So many things could go wrong at the beach, out in the middle of all that ... sand. So many mishaps could happen in the middle of a museum. So many cataclysms could occur during the occasional trip to the library.

The possibilities are endless, and you must be certifiably prepared for everything. It's a good thing you spent a full week during pregnancy shopping for the perfect diaper bag. Your diaper bag with carefully crafted pockets to carry everything. Pockets that zip shut so you don't lose anything. Pockets that are filled with all of the baby things that you think you'll need but will never use. Baby things, like twenty diapers for a two-hour outing.

And why wouldn't you fill it to the brim? You never know what could happen. You live life in a heightened state of preparedness now that you have a child. You'll never be thrown for a loop.

Baby sunscreen? Check. Extra wipes? Check. Unicorn tears to protect from the harsh realities of life? Fuck! So much for a healthy childhood.

Overpacking ... Just To Go To The Store

The fear is real. And it grabs you. What will people possibly think if you're not perfectly prepared for every possible situation? Will they tell you you're a bad parent? Will they tell you your child is suffering unnecessarily? Will they tell you those things all because you forgot to refill the antiseptic wipes you use on shopping cart handles?

Yes.

The eyes of judgment are upon you. Flying around your head are the whispers of helicopter parents. Slowly prowling and ready to pounce are the tiger moms and dads with their awful teeth, claws, and roars of death. As you recoil with fear, you'll find the fit moms yelling in your ear, telling you that there are no excuses, in all of their inspirational fit-mom glory.

Deep down, you probably think that a few germs wouldn't hurt anyone, but you don't dare say that out loud. The vicious culture of parenting surrounds you on all sides. Watch out. Never relax. You must be prepared for everything. You never know when you'll be unassumingly asked for moisturizing hand wipes, only to discover it was a secret test by an agent of the local Playground Mafia to see if you have what it takes. Do you? They'll let you know if you don't.

Once You Have It Figured Out

The inevitable is bound to happen ... multiple times, in fact. You'll have your routine in place. You'll become comfortable with it. You'll spice it up every once and a while. You'll think, "I've got this down." Then, boom! a milestone smacks you in the face, and everything you thought you knew, everything you thought you had figured out— everything in your life—will get thrown out the window, and you'll start again from scratch.

Teething, rolling, crawling, teething, walking, talking, teething, solid foods, teething ... each one will throw your routine down the drain and turn on the garbage disposal, destroying life as you know it ... again.

That's another dirty secret of parenting. Naive newbies will get a couple of months into the quest and say something like, "I think I have the hang of this."

The seasoned vets will reply with something like, "Oh good, that's great to hear."

You'll nod and smile—you're a part of the club now. The Playground Mafia has accepted you. You've become a parenting master. They're giving it to you straight. Your more experienced parent friends wouldn't put you on, would they?

You know the answer to this! Yes, they would. Parents will lie to your face just for their own amusement. You're just the local jester. They set you up to watch as you plunge into the water, unexpectedly, like in a dunk tank. Dunked by the first round of teething. It's a shock.

But you still don't believe this. You don't believe your friends will set you up. Not them. They are nice. They build you up. They encourage you to relax. You just professed you've got this parenting thing on lock, and they agreed. You trust them.

You'll find out. Secretly, they're just counting down the days until the dunking happens. They gleefully anticipate the moment they hear you say, "What the fuck?! I thought I had it all figured out."

Chapter 10

THE PARENTING PERSPECTIVE

As you grew up, you learned that there is an appropriate way and place to deal with and direct your less-than-happy emotions. You learn to blame your parents ... for everything. It's all their fault.

Remember that time you got way too drunk in college and slept through your final? Your parents' fault. Remember that time you flopped on the most important job interview you ever had? Your parents' fault. Remember that time you tried to make a romantic dinner at home and gave your date food poisoning? Your parents' fault.

It's all their fault. And because you experienced their faultiness in all its glory, you're not going to make the same mistakes. You're going to be better than they were. No more rules. No more time-outs. No more limits on Halloween candy. You're never going to miss a game.

You're never going to be grumpy. You're never going to make the same awful mistakes that put you at such a disadvantage in life, right? Of course not.

Parenting to fix the pains of your childhood is always a great perspective to parent from. In fact, the more you take the past into consideration and let it dominate your every move and thought, the better chance you have at correcting it. Dealing with the past—by going to therapy or by just getting over it—isn't helpful. If you move on, how can you make sure you'll make a change? So what's the solution? To parent from trauma.

Parenting from trauma is only possible if you're trapped in it. Endow your child with all of the traumatic experiences of your life. Treat them not like they're your child, but like they are you. You won't mess yourself up like your parents did. You'll be a superhero in your child's eyes. You'll be a superhero until you die. You'll never make a mistake. You'll never be like them.

Until you are.

Little by little, you'll realize you are much closer to becoming your parents than you thought you were. Little by little, it will happen. You'll say something to your child and remember a grudge that you still hold against your own parents. A grudge from a time you behaved like a child and they said the same thing to you that you are currently uttering to your child. Finally, you'll come to one of two conclusions: Either you're awful like your parents were, or maybe, just maybe, your mom and dad were not that bad after all.

Wouldn't that be something? Maybe they were right to put you in time-out for eating all of the cookies from the cookie jar.

Parenting shifts perspective from the child's perspective to the parenting perspective. And it's a mindfuck.

My So-Called Perfect Sibling

Siblings are a problem that not everyone is lucky enough to have. Especially older siblings. Not everyone is lucky enough to have an older sibling. Older siblings who rub it in your tearful face that life is easy. Older siblings who remind you that they have multiple kids, and a social life, and a career, and that they do it all with ease. Older siblings that remind you that you're not them.

Your sibling is a liar, just like when you were six and they lied about who ripped a hole in Mom's dress.

Don't let your sibling pull the ol' *you're not cut out for this like me* wool over your eyes.

Older siblings are just larger versions of who they were in childhood: annoying assholes. They rub it in that they had three kids under five. They rub it in that they work full time, not because they need the job, but solely because they want to rub it in your face. They rub it in that they cook dinner for the family from scratch every night. They rub it in that after all of that, they still have time for a daily run and yoga. It makes you want to vomit every time they open their mouth.

"It couldn't be that hard. You only have one."

"Oh please, I can do it all with ease. Put in some effort."

"How do you not have this all under control?"

Comments like that are weapons of war. Warfare that's expected from the extended family, not from a loving sibling. A loving, older sibling who would never be childish enough to use your parenting abilities to continue a grudge they've held for decades. Siblings don't do that.

But if they do, remind them that the ease of parenting, of which *they* speak, must be the reason *their* kids behave so well.

One point for you. You've won the first round of the Fami-Royale. Doesn't it feel good?

The Extended Family ... Drama

It's not just the siblings who will psychologically bomb you. The extended family is like a state-sponsored terrorist organization, ready to beat you into submission in front of the world.

No matter what you do, it's wrong. In fact, the only time you're not wrong is when they talk and you agree. But every time you agree, a little piece of your soul dies a horrible death. Yet you agree with your extremist family just to avoid an argument at Grandma's eighty-third birthday extravaganza. It's the family event of the year that you couldn't possibly miss, because for some ~~stupid~~ reason, eighty-three is a milestone in your family.

There you are, sitting across from Uncle Chuck, who is only three years older than you, and Aunt Bertha, who is two years younger and acts like she's next in line to be the family's matriarch, because she and your uncle started popping out kids when she was eighteen, and now they have seven.

Secretly, you hate them all.

Family dinner time makes you want to scream because Uncle Chuck and Aunt Bertha were too busy doing the nasty to teach their kids table manners. And because of the sounds those disgusting little terrors make, you never eat at these family functions, and then you get lectured. You get the lecture from Bertha that you're too skinny, despite the fact you feel awful because of the vanilla-latte-a-day forty you've gained, which you mention. That mention starts Bertha on a tirade, and she gets the family involved.

Now you've got thirty-five members of your extended family trying to convince you to eat some pie. Thirty-five members of your family tell you if you don't take care of yourself by eating a plate full of food and multiple desserts, your child will suffer. Then, they'll go on and say that it looks like your child *is* suffering, at least compared to the other cousins. And there you are, slowly nodding and agreeing just to get them to shut the fuck up because you don't have the energy to argue with the entire extended family for the entire trip.

Then, just when you think it's over, just when you're about to leave ... you get one last guilt trip about how no one ever sees you. You hear, "Come visit more often. It's been so great having you here."

For who? Not you. Yet, you smile and say, "Oh, we'll have to fix that."

Now you're on the hook for the next awful gathering.

Back home, after the eleven-hour trip, you close the front door and take a deep breath. As you do, your mother calls. She's not happy. You find out that you were rude and smug. You find out that Auntie Bertha's feelings were hurt and Uncle Chuck was very disappointed in his little munchkin. Your mother goes on to tell you that she has received multiple calls about your uppity "new parent" behavior—whatever the fuck that means—and that maybe you should think about getting it in check before the next gathering, which you *are* expected to be at. Maybe at that point, you'll be mature enough to apologize to the family for the disgrace you have brought on them.

That's what you have to look forward to next month when you go home. There is no quick fix for extended family drama. With one exception ...

Ghost them all. Don't go, and stop responding to everyone. They'll eventually get the hint. Really they won't—they'll talk about you every time they get together—but you won't have to hear about it.

Ultimately, it's your choice. You can either engage in the extended family drama or not. Either way, it's one of those universal laws: The only family members who like family gatherings are the family members you don't like.

Good luck with that.

Friends Who Just Don't Get It

It's easy to see why friends, particularly childless ones, don't get it. There's a huge shift that takes place when you have a demanding kid attached to you for most of the day. If your friends are normal, they'll fit into a few categories.

The first is the naive version of your snarky sibling. This is the friend who has good intentions, but those intentions highlight the rift between you and your old life. This friend tries to include you. They invite you out on a Wednesday night for drinks. Then they say, "Why not? What do you have going on?"

This is the friend who tells you, "Buck up. It's not that hard. You only need to eat better, exercise, and get some sleep."

See? Naive version of your snarky sibling.

Then there's the friend who is the worst liar in the world. This friend is the one who tries to put you on but fails. The conversation goes something like, "It's you! You look fantastic. You're so ... robust. And your outfit, it's so ... casual 90s. You know, when I'm a parent, I'm going to be such an inspiration. No one is going to accuse me of letting myself slide. So, there's the baby ... what else is going on in your life?"

You answer, "Not much else going on in my life right now."

Your friend chuckles and says, "You're so funny."

You think, "I hate you so much right now." Except that you're so tired, you actually say it out loud and don't give a fuck.

And because you don't give a fuck, your friend laughs and says, "I love this new edge, It's so George Costanza."

Then it hits you. An inspiration? Letting yourself slide? You realize that your best friend secretly thinks you let yourself go but can't muster up the heart to say anything. And it's shattering. You start to ask if that means you look like a middle-aged, balding man, but you stop yourself. You stop yourself because it's not worth it. They are trying. Bless them—they try. But they fail miserably.

There is also the friend who you thought would be really good with your child, but in reality, doesn't want a thing to do with them. They back away from your family and shut you out. You become aware that your child makes them feel awkward. Your child brings up long-buried childhood trauma. When you ask them about it, you realize your friend blames you. After all, you're the one who had the child. How dare you not take their repressed childhood trauma into consideration.

And finally, there is the type of friend who is great with your kid. They're easy-going and fun. They know how to help with the basics like feedings and diapers, bathing and bedtime. But they have the worst mouth imaginable. The G-rated version of their vocabulary is a master class in profanity usage for most. But you don't know what to do because you're miserable, and this friend is a legit help. They know more about the baby than your partner. They actually make life easier. But fucking hell, can't they tone it down?

You start to worry your child will get kicked out of pre-school for cussing out the entire class *and* teaching staff. When you say something to your friend, they tell you you've become a prude. They tell you it goes over your child's head. What are you complaining about? They're helping you. They'll tone it down in a few years.

Except they don't.

Hanging out with your childless friends becomes something you do less and less. The divide becomes greater and greater. It hurts. You put all the blame on them. After all, they made new friends. They planned trips to the places you fantasized together about. They have great nights out at your old favorite spots and post photos about it. They live the life you were supposed to live together. Without you.

They move on because they don't know how to relate to your new life. They move on because they think you've filled a void. They move on because you moved on.

Childless friends just don't get it. They can't. It's truly a perspective shift that you can only appreciate by having a kid. People will argue otherwise. They're wrong. They'll learn for themselves when they have a kid.

CENSORING LIFE

Some of your friends will harmlessly drop an f-bomb or two every couple of minutes. But an f-bomb is nothing like the crazy shit you'll see on the streets of any big city. It's also nothing like the extreme, right-wing, socially conservative, religious cultism you'll get in other parts of the country.

The world is full of crazy. You'll have the impulse to keep your child safe from all the whack jobs you encounter along the way, as you should. But as your kid grows older, you'll need to prepare them to fend off the crazy on their own.

You don't want your naive, innocent, legal adult running off to college primed to pop Quaaludes, do lines of coke in the bathroom before hitting up the gym, or challenge Grant the Human Beer Truck to a drinking contest, do you? You also don't want your kid landing on the street, insulting everyone who walks by because they've been stuck in a bubble for eighteen years and haven't realized there are other ways to live ... or do you? You don't want your kid giving away all of the money you sent them to supplement their unpaid internship to the local junkie on the corner who fell on hard times and only needs a few more bucks to finally get back on their feet, do you? No, you don't!

You want your kid to understand that there are major problems in the world, but that there are proper avenues to fix them. You also want your child to understand that some people are out for themselves and will get what they want by any means necessary. Not everyone is cut from the same cloth, and your child needs to learn that while they are growing up under the protection and guidance of their parents.

You want your child to grow up understanding how to keep the crazy at bay on their own.
But to do that, they need to understand that crazy exists. Pretending that it doesn't does your child a disservice.

So the next time you see a group of naked, elderly men standing at a bus stop, smoking meth, and your kid asks, "Why are they naked?" ... just remember your friend who drops the occasional f-bomb. That f-bomb doesn't seem so bad now, does it?

Re-Asking For Help

Friends and family are well intentioned, but sometimes they'll forget about you. They'll forget about you because they have their own lives. Go figure.

So ask for help. Again. Then don't take it personally if you have to ask again. And again. And again.

And if they ignore you for months and basically disappear ... then they're not much of a friend, are they?

People Who Disappear

People disappear after you have kids. It's hard not to take it personally, especially since your new addition was the catalyst for your friends' disappearance. But it happens, and like a bad breakup ... it's not you, it's them.

Prepare yourself now. Some people will ghost you. You can never predict who it might be, but you *can* prepare yourself that it will happen. When it does, it's going to burn. It's going to hurt. Ultimately, you're better off without them.

Do you really have the time and energy to waste on people who don't reciprocate? Who are disinterested? No, you don't. However, you can relish in the fact that if *they* ever have kids, some of their friends will leave them, just like they left you.

While it hurts, try to remember they're probably hanging out with hipsters, sitting around complaining about the hardship of jadedness.

Dog Parents

Some of your friends will equate having a dog to having a kid. They call themselves dog parents.

They'll talk about how the trip to the pound is just like pregnancy. That the day their dog came home from the kennel was just like giving birth. They'll equate filling up a dog bowl with kibble and changing the water once every few days to feeding an infant ... every four hours. They'll argue that early morning walks and the occasional puppy accident on the kitchen floor are equal to ten to twelve diapers a day. They'll come into work and complain that their new puppy was scared of the dark last night and that it's just like sleep training. They'll tell you that the added responsibility of taking care of a living being, which they get to leave in the house most of the day, has made them understand what parents go through.

Fuck dog parents.

That felt good.

Chapter 11

Birthday Brats

Ah, birthdays. Celebrating the little natural disaster that destroyed your life as you knew it.

Birthdays are a tricky event to find balance with. Too little celebration, and the kid, for whom you have graciously provided the other three hundred and sixty-four days of the year, will grow up believing you didn't care and will resent you for the remainder of their life. They'll resent you while they attend their friends' celebrations year after year. Friends who had parents who did care, and who showed it by throwing extravagant celebrations. Extravagant celebrations that continue into adulthood to commemorate milestone ages like thirty-four or twenty-six.

On the other side of the coin, if you celebrate the fuck out of your kid's birthday each year, they'll turn into monsters. You'll have destroyed their chance at growing up to be a decent individual. Celebrate too much, and you'll wonder for the rest of your life, "How did I raise such an asshole?"

Birthdays. That's how.

But there you are. You didn't heed the warning. You threw an extravagant annual event in reaction to FOFUYCL. You gathered a group of people for a stressful smorgasbord to reinforce the idea that the world revolves around your kid. It's understandable. You feel like you're damaging your child if they only have themes, decorations, cakes, activities, and a plethora of presents. To stop the potential damage, you rent bouncy houses and bowling alleys, movie theaters and amusement parks. You hire adults who dress up as imaginary characters and magicians. You have ponies and bubbles and face paint. You hire a mermaid for the pool you had put in for the party.

Year after year, right before your eyes, you watch your kid become a self-centered brat. In the months leading up to their birthday, you watch them figure out that they run shit. You watch as they figure out that all will bow to their will and kiss the ring. You anxiously anticipate any sort of potential discomfort in order to ensure that the illusion of ruling the world is never broken.

Your FOFUYCL is your demise.

One day, you'll be old and alone in an old folks' home because your child didn't have the time to deal with you. You'll sit there and gaze out the window, and you'll think about where it all went wrong. You'll trace it back to the birthday with the forty-year-old man dressed up as a Jedi or the one with the fifty-year-old mermaid who liked bubbles. There, in your final home, while you and your new social group silently eat Jell-O, you'll suddenly yell out, "Fuck bubbles and bouncy houses. Fuck birthdays! Fuck birthdays!!!!"

Like sloths, your friends will slowly turn and look at you as the ~~orderlies~~ nurses wheel you away to have private time. You're disturbing the nurses' lunch break. A break they use to plan their own child's birthday extravaganza.

Don't get wheeled away. Get the birthdays in check now.

Holiday Drama

The holidays. Proof that the human race as a species is masochistic. What torture. What stress and strife. What pointlessness. It's all absurd. We withhold gifts and kind gestures from our friends and loved ones for an entire year, and then one day, after months of pressure to buy the perfect gift, after months of pressure to fulfill unfulfillable expectations, we give those gifts that we've been withholding. As long as everyone behaves.

Why? Why not spread the gifts out over the course of a year and use them as good-behavior bribes? Bribery is the gift that keeps on giving. Why blow it all on one day?

Hands down, the worst thing about the holidays is the pressure. The pressure to make everyone happy. The pressure to be everywhere. The pressure to be merry. It comes from all angles.

Then there are the events and gatherings with everyone under the sun. Your family, your in-laws, your friends, your kid's school—everyone has something going on. Those somethings revolve around the same songs, the same stories, the same food, the same drinks, and the same arguments about the same shit from the prior year. Those arguments result in the same insults, the same tears, and the same false apologies.

Then there is pressure to get something meaningful. And the pressure to get the latest and greatest thing. When you have a kid, all of that is magnified. Remember how hard it was to find the balance for the birthday extravaganza? The holidays are that, times a million. Everyone will get your kid something. There will be more presents under the tree than ever before. The glossy paper and pretty bows promising the greatest holiday ever.

And after the storm passes and all is calm, you know what your kid will play with? The empty boxes. The empty boxes and the new squeaky toy for Aunt Bertha's dog, who is too lazy to chew it.

The holidays are awful. How do you win?

SETTING BOUNDARIES

You set boundaries. You set boundaries with regard to everything.

Spell it out. Who is going to see your child, and who isn't? You get to choose. Let them all know that you're the new parent. Tell them all what you're doing and what you're not. You have the baby. It's most inconvenient for you. Take the initiative and make it convenient for yourself. If they don't like it, they'll get over it. There are three hundred and sixty-four other days of the year to see you. It doesn't all have to happen on one day.

Part of setting boundaries is resetting the expectations of others. It's not your responsibility to save the holidays for everyone by showing up at x time and y place with the kid in tow.

Make them come to you. And bring all the food. And do all the cleanup. The holidays are the perfect time to practice telling those around you what you need.

Set boundaries. Keep the crazy out.

TRAVELING AND SCHEDULING

No doubt you'll get the ol' "You're going to be over at noon for dinner, aren't you?" Or, "You're going to bring your family across the country, with all the baby things, right? We really don't feel like traveling."

If you're down with that, then do it. But if you don't want to travel, then don't travel. Do your own thing. Start your own traditions. Call your family's bluff and make them come out to you ... but only if you want them to. What matters is being true to your own family unit.

RESETTING BOUNDARIES

You'll get pushback from your family. They'll tell you their holiday happiness is tied to your presence. They'll let you know their holiday happiness is tied to seeing your child on a certain day at a certain time. They'll say that they won't know how to forgive you if you don't show up for yams and ham with Uncle Chuck and Aunt Bertha. They'll play hardball. They'll threaten to not visit. They'll threaten to not send anything.

Good. Tell them not to send anything. And don't visit. Do you want to teach your kid to be subservient to your extended family's every last wish? Your happiness is your responsibility. Their happiness is theirs.

If they don't come out, less stress for you. You can use the money you'll save on a babysitter.

BUT WON'T MY CHILD SUFFER?

The short answer? No.

The long answer? Your kid needs to learn about perspective. The holidays are set up to blow balance and perspective out of the water. No one gets everything, including your extended family. That's not to say that deprivation is the road to happiness, balance, and perspective. Be a warm beer on a cold day. That's balance personified. That's not personification per se, but you get the point.

Civilization has been around for thousands of years. If excess and getting your way all the time were the keys to happiness, there would be a saying about it. There isn't. Set boundaries. Find balance. Tell the extended family what your immediate family needs. Then let it all go. Stressing about it doesn't solve anything.

Besides, who wants to spend an entire day with Aunt Bertha, her kids, and her lazy fucking dog, whom she calls Kid Number Eight?

Warm beer on a cold day.

Chapter 12

DEALING WITH THE MILESTONES

As the months come and go, you'll notice that more and more milestones come to pass, each fucking up your routine and leaving your life splattered all over the kitchen floor. You'll want to quit.

As you start to quit, you must remember that this is your quest. Your quest will have its ups and downs. Everything is temporary. You will muster up the energy to get to the top of the hill. When you reach the top of this hill, you'll see paradise in front of you.

Except that's not true. When you get to the top of the hill, you'll see an entire mountain range in front of you. Paradise is a long way off. Which is why you *should* quit.

Quit. Please, quit. Quit trying to control the present. Quit hoping for a certain future to happen. It won't. Kids don't operate in your fantasy world. The sooner you quit trying to control the present and the future, the sooner you quit trying to fix your past, the sooner you quit wasting energy complaining about how hard it is ... the sooner you'll be able to accept that this is life. Life is change. Milestones lead to change. Change that deep down you don't really want, but guess what? Nobody cares. Life doesn't revolve around you anymore. You are just a speck in a larger picture.

Change happens. That's just life.

Teaching Your Kid How To Do Things

Now that you've miraculously embraced change and given up control, you're ready to move forward. You're ready to enjoy everything that change has to offer. You're ready to embrace your inner sadist. You're ready to take what life dishes out and smile.

Because you've embraced your inner sadist and are now enjoying the hell out of change, you get to deal with all of the fun rites of passage that take you out of baby town and into big kid land.

You get to teach your kid how to form sentences and eat with silverware. You get to potty train and teach them how to throw trash in the trash can. You get to teach them about animals and numbers and letters and shapes. You get to teach them how to flip people off. Then you get to teach them that flipping people off is only for adults, that kids don't do that ... but only after you capture it on video. Because it's hilarious. You teach them about what is fair and what isn't. You teach them how to be polite.

Or you don't. Not every segment of the population values the same ideas. You get to teach them that. Or not. Some people feel like they should teach their kid that it's their way or the highway. The point is, once you get over the need for normalcy and start to enjoy change, you'll start having fun. You'll start moving forward out of the torturous land of failed expectations.

Change will happen. The sooner you embrace it, the less tired, frustrated, and emotionally wiped out you'll be.

THE TERRIBLE TWOS MYTH

Terrible twos. It's a myth. A myth of epic proportions.

Yes, you deal with tantrums, and lots of energetic, erratic running around, but overall, two is not that bad. As you've learned by now, parents are liars. It's fun to set up naive, new parents for disappointment.

You'll see. You'll get through two and say something like, "It wasn't that bad. I've got this."

Your parent friends will smile at you and say, "Of course, you do. You've got this now."

But they know. They know that in a matter of a few weeks, maybe even days, your child is going to turn into a bratty, mouthy asshole. It happens around a specific milestone. And your friends will be there to celebrate, basking in the transformation.

Third Birthday: Where Did My Kid Go?

There is a secret, evil island in the middle of the ocean of lost hopes and dreams. On that island, there is a top secret machine that will seek out your child when they turn three years old. That machine will suck out all the good, sweet behavior from your child and leave nothing but awful tantrums, sass, and pure crappiness until they turn four. The crappiness left behind will turn your child into a little monster. That little monster will hit you, smash toys, break all of your favorite things, and tell you that they do not love you anymore, all over the course of a typical evening.

Now occasionally, the machine located on the secret, evil island will break, and you'll have moments where the goodness returns. Those moments will be brief and fleeting. You'll be in the middle of dinner, having a great time with Grandma, and all of a sudden you'll catch a piece of chicken tender in the face, followed by half a glass of milk spilled on the shirt you got from Grandma. All on purpose.

While you stare at the milk dripping onto the floor, you'll have a flood of emotions. Sadness, defeat, anger, and sadistic happiness because you hated that shirt anyway. None of that will matter. No matter how you react, you're just along for the ride, Hold on tight. It's a doozy. Only one thing can stop the ride. Only one thing can stop the machine from sucking all the goodness away from your once little angel, and it's not some boring book.

Time. Time will stop the machine on the secret, evil island. You see, the machine doesn't work on four-year-olds. There is light at the end of the tunnel.

FOURNADO?

Here's the thing: When the machine runs for such a long time, it creates a vacuum. When it turns off on your kid's fourth birthday party, a rush of goodness hits your child like a windstorm. The windstorm is accompanied by an eerie light. The light has a gray tint. It feels like a storm. A storm called the Fournado. That storm is a fucking monster.

The Fournado is like a tornado that's smart. It looks for your weaknesses and knows exactly how to exploit them. If it sees an opening, it will pounce. Anything it can do to fuck up your day and get a reaction, it will do.

"Oh look, Mommy doesn't want me to drop water on the floor during bath time. I wonder how mad can I make her if I dump a cup full of water on the floor?"

"Oh look, Daddy wants me to eat breakfast before school. I'll see how mad he gets if I drag out eating an egg and toast for an hour and a half."

"Oh, what's that, Mommy and Daddy? You want me to go up to my room for time-out? Fine. I don't like you and was already going there anyway to have a time-out from you."

Luckily, just like a tornado, the Fournado fizzles out quickly. One day you'll notice in front of you a walking, talking, calm, imaginative, little person. You'll notice it's been weeks since the last storm.

At first, you'll be shell-shocked. You'll wait for the other shoe to drop. You'll wonder when the gig is up. You'll deal with a brief fit and think you're back in the trenches. But you're not. You made it through.

Chapter 13

New Influences

Once upon a time, there was SuperParent and a helpless little child. That little child needed guidance. That little child needed guidance in a world of chaos, destruction, and sleep deprivation. SuperParent battled with teething, solid foods, colds, walking, talking, playground dynamics, and holidays. SuperParent battled against the extended family and even defeated the evil, two-headed Chuck-and-Bertha Monster.

But then one day, the helpless little child became restless and was in need of socialization. And so SuperParent embarked upon the most important mission of the year: new influences.

Setting Up Your Kid For Success

Hopefully, you're one of those parents who wants what's best for their child. You want your child to grow up to achieve happiness and success, no matter what they set their minds to. You want your child to live a life worth talking about and worth exaggerating until it becomes a mythical quest, a beacon of light for all others to follow. But for your kid to be all they can be, they need to be set up for success.

Setting up your kid for success, like everything else, isn't easy. It's counterintuitive. Your first impulse is to give your kid everything and help them out whenever you can. You buy the best equipment. You pay for lessons with the best teachers money can buy. You help with projects, read them books, and do their homework if they have too much. You don't want your kid to struggle.

But your kid needs to struggle. They need to learn that failure is okay. They need to learn how they learn. They need to learn that Mommy and Daddy won't always be there to help them with every step of life. They need to learn that if you shake up a can of beer before you open it, it will spray everywhere.

Your goal is to help them build confidence. They need enough help to keep going and enough support that failure isn't crippling. You need to learn when to push them and when to cut them slack.

Of course, just like everything else in your life, as you start to make progress, it gets destroyed by the next milestone in life: school.

And everything that goes with it.

School ... Other Kids ... And Teachers

You'd think it would be a great thing for your child to start school. Though you might be sad, that little energy suck will finally be out of the house and on its own ... at least for a few hours a day.

As soon as you pick them up from their new social circle though, you'll notice a change. A big change. Your kid will realize, over those few short hours, that you are no longer the be-all, end-all authority in their lives. Their new best friends are. And because they are wired for social acceptance, they'll start doing whatever it takes, which means bringing home new phrases and adopting new behaviors. Guess what? There is nothing you can do about it.

To top it off, they see their teachers every day, and you'll soon hear three words that will undercut your authority for the remainder of your years: *my teacher said ...*

Yep. Teachers and their fucking authority issues. You

give a child a good home, and food, and shelter, and love
... and what thanks do you get? A demotion in status and
a nice, daily reminder that in your child's eyes, your
knowledge is useless. You might have a PhD, but to your
kid, you're no better than the town idiot. You're a jester.

For you, every day your kid is at school is another day
further down the path of idiocy. Oh, you're an expert in
your field? Who gives a shit. Oh, you stay up to date on
current events? You are not a reliable source! Oh, you're
interested in learning something new? You should ask
you kid's teacher for suggestions. They know everything.

Welcome back to school. It's back to wreck your life ...
again.

KIDS WHO BEHAVE LIKE BRATS

Some of the kids you'll meet over the next few years are
going to be a great influence. They are going to teach your
little angel a lot and be there throughout life as voices of
encouragement and cohorts in harmless trouble. They'll
forever be tied to memories of joy.

There will also be babies, bullies, and brats. Those are the
worst. They're the worst because not only will they challenge your child, they'll also test your own self-control.

You'll catch yourself thinking absolutely detestable thoughts about those four-year-olds. You'll find yourself not only thinking awful thoughts about those kids, but also endowing the brats' parents with the worst qualities imaginable.

You'll try to be an adult, though. You'll encourage your kid to play with other kids and leave the bullies to their own accord. If that doesn't work, you'll tell the teacher and yourself that little Timmy is rough around the edges. But to your dismay, that won't work either. Then one fateful day, you'll go to a school event and see little Timmy push your child, and you'll snap. Your voice will drop an octave, and you'll bark out, "Leave my kid alone!"

Mission accomplished. That little fuck is shocked, and your child is ~~only partially embarrassed~~ relieved. You give the kid the evil eye and growl, and he runs. Finally, you breathe a sigh of relief. You finally did what Timmy's parents couldn't.

Until little Timmy cries, and the parent, who turns out to be a feeble, widowed grandpa, hobbles over to ask you what your problem is. You'll start to justify your behavior, but you'll get shut down when Grandpa explains that Timmy's parents died in a car accident, and he's having trouble dealing with it.

Who's the bratty asshole now?

But there's one more plot twist.

Grandpa was lying. Timmy's parents are alive and well. Grandpa just secretly thinks you and your child are the real bullies, and he told little Timmy it was okay to stand up for himself and punch your kid in the arm. To thicken the plot even more, what your child left out in this manipulative tale of woe is that the conflict started when your kid yelled, "Timmy, you're a fatty!"

What is the lesson here? All kids behave like brats at one time or another. Your kid isn't an exception to the rule.

The other lesson? Grandparents are parents too, and they have much more practice at lying than you do.

SCHOOL PARENTS

Speaking of adults ... there is another factor that you'll deal with when your child gets to school: parents.

School parents are the worst. They're demanding and hypersensitive and opinionated. They're competitive and ready to put others down so they can jockey for position as Supreme Parent.

In the real world, it's all about your social standing. Who is at the top of the food chain? Who are the trend setters and natural leaders? Who is the most capable room parent? That doesn't change in school. Because everything revolves around kids, it's all magnified.

So prepare yourself. When school starts, you'll feel like you are in middle school on steroids. Focus on the prize. Your job is to help your kid gather the tools needed to survive while you try to survive your own prolonged adult middle-school drama. If you can both get through that, high school will be a breeze.

Good luck.

Chapter 14

THE GOLDEN AGE

Once your kid makes it through the secret, evil island, the Fournado, and learns how to navigate school, you'll find yourself in a very comfortable spot: The Golden Age.

The Golden Age is the stage of parenting that every parent dreams of. If you do your job, provide love and the right amount of structure, and keep major threats at bay, you'll get a few solid years of what are, hands down, the best years of parenting.

It isn't an overnight transition. One day you will wake up and realize that you have gradually moved into a relationship with a little person. It's amazing. Once you realize that, you'll instantly forget the years of strife. You'll be flooded with more love than ever for your child.

It is pure bliss ...

The Second Time Around

And because The Golden Age is pure bliss, you'll want it to continue. You'll start to chase it. Obsess over it. You'll bring up having another child with your partner, forgetting that the two of you barely made it the first time around. No matter—it's easy to dismiss the negativity when you're pumped full of oxytocin. You've completely forgotten all the anguish you've been through over the past few years.

So, you'll drunkenly pose the question to your partner one night. You'll both agree, and without sobering up, or asking questions like "Can we afford this?" or "Can our partnership afford this?" or "Can our own emotional life afford this?" ... you'll use a little red wine as liquid impulsiveness, and after four and a half minutes of pure bliss, you'll blast right back to the start of your quest.

Maybe you should have sobered up. Maybe you should have had a conversation after the moment of passion. But you didn't, and now it's all over.

It's fine. You'll lie to yourself and make up a new set of naive expectations just like the first time. You'll say things like:

"It'll be easier this time!"

"I know what I'm doing now!"

"It's going to be so different. I'll use everything I learned from the first child straight out of the gate for the second kid."

It's so cyclical. It's so serendipitous. You're a little further along, yet you're still in the same place you were for the first one—believing a bunch of bullshit.

That's what happens when you get a taste of The Golden Age. It's intoxicating. And you won't want it to end.

Life is a travesty. It's got such a sick sense of humor.

Chapter 15

It's Not "One Size Fits All"

Just like a bra or shoes, parenting is not "one size fits all." Your child, your family needs, your values, your experiences, your traumas, your doubts, your joyous moments ... they're all unique. A uniqueness that, regardless of what this book says, means you, your child, and your family have your own challenges that will drastically change your parenting experience. That's the nature of life—no matter what, there will always be outliers. And it's probably you.

You're going to be flooded with information, and (unlike what the beginning of the book says) there is no roadmap for your quest. It'll be up to you to sift through the information, opinions, and judgments to figure out what works for you. It's about you and your family, not about the opinions of Uncle Chuck and Aunt Bertha.

Conflicts will arise. Buttons will be pushed. Tempers and frustrations will flare. Tears will fall. Joy will radiate from your every pore. It will all happen again and again. Things will change, and as soon as you learn to cope with whatever is currently going on, things will change again.

Most of the time, parenting will be inconvenient. At the beginning, it will feel endless and isolating. You'll wonder where the old you went. The old you won't return. They're gone. But if you put in the work, a new you will emerge from your quest, and that new you will have such an understanding of humanity, such a greater appreciation for life, that you won't think twice about the old you or your old life.

Having a child is counterintuitive to the philosophy of modern culture. There is no healthy form of instant gratification in parenting. What you think is a good choice in the moment could very well land you eating pudding in a nursing home later in life. If you're in it for the long haul, then you can find what works for your family. Your family is what matters more than anything else in the world ... make sure you include yourself.

Your Kid Learns From The Examples You Set

Your kids learn from you. They watch you all the time. They don't give a damn what you say, especially if you behave differently. The beauty of kids is that you don't have to be perfect to be good for them. They'll take you as you are. They'll see when you try your best. They'll see when you put your best foot forward. Show them how you deal with adversity. Teach them to learn from missteps and failures. Show them that there is no such thing as perfect. Teach them that bad things will happen and that those bad things will pass. Teach them to appreciate the good, because it won't last forever.

Teach them all of this by trying your best to live it yourself. Watching you live is how they learn the most. They might learn information from their teachers, but they learn to walk in *your* footsteps.

Just A Reminder: Not Everyone Should Be A Parent

Not everyone should be a parent, and hopefully you honestly asked yourself that before you started on your quest. If you didn't, you're still on the hook to provide a good childhood for your kid. It's your job to find a way to replace what you can't give.

It's still your job to be a parent, even if you figured out you're an awful one.

HAVING A CHILD DOESN'T MEAN LIFE IS OVER

Parents are liars. They want you to think that life is over if you have a kid. They do that because parents know how difficult parenting is. They want to scare away those who shouldn't be parents. The truth is, once your kid is in school, there will be a lot of time for you to be who you want to be. Life doesn't stop because you've had a child; it expands ... out of the dive bars you've been used to.

JUDGMENTAL FUCKS

Most parents are perpetually looking out for the well-being of every child they come across. Sometimes, when they express that concern, they come across as judgmental fucks. You, at some point, will come across as a judgmental fuck. Parents fall into the trap of looking at life through their own skewed lens. They adamantly give advice, which might never apply to your life. The good intentions are there, though.

Try to remember: It's not about cutting you down; it's about protecting your kid's childhood. Kids deserve a chance to succeed. That chance is bigger than your ego. That chance is worth the risk of being a judgmental fuck.

Your Happiness ... Is Your Responsibility

It's easy in this day and age to feel like everyone else is to blame. It's easy to make excuses for not doing something. It's easy to get trapped in the pity party merry-go-round. It's also easy to get out.

Once you realize that your happiness is your responsibility, then there is nothing that can stop you. It can also have a lasting impact on how your kid views life. Once you take action, instead of waiting to be saved, you become the master of your own destiny. Once you figure that out, your quest can take a joyful turn and become a glittering beacon of life and light—not some sad, woe-is-me existence, where your happiness is dependent upon everyone else's approval.

It all starts with you. Are you ready for the greatest quest of your life? Or would you like to stay in prison, dreaming about a life worth living, like Don Quixote?

Start A Playground Mafia

Quests are hard to go at alone. It's important to find a group of people with whom you can be honest about all of the seedy parts of parenting life. Building a Playground Mafia is easier than you think. You can take classes. Or try this magical phrase when you pass someone as you push your stroller in a desperate attempt to warm your coffee and charge your phone:

"Hi! How are you?"

It's a novel phrase. It weeds out the parents who will ultimately create the little Timmy's of the world from those who are worthwhile. You'll know it's a match if the person gives you the greatest gift you can get in the Playground Mafia: an answer with heartfelt honesty and humor.

Heartfelt honesty and humor—a lot of humor—are the language of the Playground Mafia. When they're at the core, your Playground Mafia becomes a safe place. A haven. A group that is shame and guilt free. A group there to support you through the hard moments and celebrate during the joyous ones. A group that doesn't add to the pressure that you're already feeling, but instead helps you live with it.

Slowly, over time, one turns into two, and two into four, and four into eight, and so on and so forth, until you have a community, a village of parents, both moms and dads, who are there for each other. A Playground Mafia of parents who earned the right to shake their heads and chuckle at the next group of new parents saying silly shit, because you, not so long ago, were right there, at the beginning of your quest saying all that silly shit too.

Be Selfish ...
Your Family Deserves Your A Game

Occasionally, because life happens on its own timing, shit will get in the way of you taking time for yourself. Days will turn into weeks, and those weeks will turn into months, and one day you'll realize that you're hanging on by a thread. In those moments, it's important to remember that you are responsible for taking care of yourself. No one is going to magically appear and save you.

Take the time. Remind yourself that it's okay to say no. Recharging is important. Especially if you're going to be a little person's hero. Your family deserves your A game, not your D game.

And one last thing ...

You're doing something incredibly hard. Be kind to yourself. You deserve it.

Bonus

SHIT HITS THE FAN

It's inevitable that shit will hit the fan. You and your partner will go through a plethora of tests. Tests that will put your relationship through the ringer. You and your partner will look out across the valley of family, from high atop a mountain, drop your guard, and start to relax, right before a killer spider crawls up your pant leg and bites you in the ass.

That bite will rock you to the core, and completely shift your perspective on life. All of a sudden, you and your partner will stop seeing eye to eye. You'll head in separate directions after arguing for months about which way to go.

When shit hits the fan, you'll have to look out for yourself and your child. All the same rules will apply in tragedy as they do in regular life. Ask for what you need. Be honest about what you don't. Try not to get stuck on a never-ending Ferris wheel of pity. Give yourself permission to feel ... everything. Don't put added pressure on yourself to be okay. Reach out to friends ... but know it's your responsibility to take care of yourself.

TRAGEDY STRIKES

We don't like to think about tragedies striking our families. Injured, sick, dying, or abused children are hard thoughts to swallow. Thoughts that we would like to keep as far away as possible. But the truth is, tragedy can happen to anyone. Tragedy doesn't discriminate. Tragedy doesn't care if you think you're a good person and don't deserve this. Tragedy doesn't bargain. Tragedy strikes when, where, and who it wants.

If tragedy strikes your family, don't go at it alone. Call someone and ask for a shoulder to cry on. Your friends will try to be there. They might say the wrong thing sometimes, but they'll try.

If that doesn't work, then there are other options for support and help. Search for a group. Find a person to talk to. Find a blog. Or a book. Something. Anything, so you know you're not alone. Take what you can from wherever you can get it and go on to the next bit. Find what you need. You make the roadmap for your quest. Not your therapist, not a TV show or a movie, not a PhD scholar. You. Don't feel the pressure to justify or explain anything. And above all, be kind to yourself—some things are out of your control.

Divorce

Divorce still brings up images of nasty domestic disputes and long, drawn-out legal battles over everything from the house and cars, to the pets and the collection of John Cougar Mellencamp T-shirts, to retirement accounts and the ashes of your first goldfish, Tito, that now reside in a stuffed monkey you named The Golden Monk. You might get the Range Rover, but you'll shed a tear over losing The Golden Monk. That's divorce. Divorce sucks. But it doesn't need to be a war.

If you're married, or were never married, or were married by your drunk friend from college who became a minister on one of those online churches and vomited halfway into the service ... going separate ways when a child is involved could very well be one of the only things harder than raising a child. It could be the most amicable breakup in the world, where you both have the best of intentions, but battling for custody can quickly become the nastiest battle you'll ever go through.

Advice? Before you have the kid, write a prenuptial agreement. You never know when something might go wrong. A prewritten agreement might just be what keeps your breakup from becoming the breakup of your night-mares. A prewritten agreement might be what you two need to start out on a path of unicorns, butterflies, and rainbows. A path of co-parenting.

Co-Parenting

Honestly, who doesn't want to have a nonadversarial, nonromantic relationship with their ex?

Many of you are blessed with exes who never want to have anything to do with you again. For the rest of you, as budding masochists ... you're gluttons for punishment. Co-parenting is that punishment.

It doesn't seem like it would be. After all, successful co-parenting is built around equality, communication, and putting aside differences for the betterment of your child and family unit—which is still there; it's just struc-tured differently. But you'll get used to the lack of con-flict. The relationship will become amicable, and you'll find yourself thinking, "Why didn't this work out? We get along great!"

The reason co-parenting works is because you keep every-thing off the table except for the kid. The ironic part is that when you were together, the kid became the only topic that was on the table. It was the topic that caused the majority of your disagreements, hurt feelings, and deep resentment. You stopped talking about everything else, which turned your relationship into a bitter partnership. And yet, here you are, discussing your child and nothing else, again, and now you're getting along better than ever. Your married friends comment about how well you get along—better than most of the married couples you know.

It works because the added pressure is gone. You no longer have the pressure to be anything. You no longer have the pressure to be the perfect family. Now you're just two people communicating about what works and what doesn't. You're two people who take care of themselves so that they can take care of their child.

Successful co-parenting comes in all forms. It's based around what works for all parties while keeping the kid's interest at heart.

Could you imagine if you had done that throughout your actual relationship? It would never have worked.

The New Normal

Finally, here you are. The end of the book. The end of your quest. Well, this part of your quest, at least. This is the end of the first book about the first part of your quest, which is honestly more of an epic, not a quest.

This book is a reaction to the Industry. It's a reaction to the shame, fear, and pressure placed on new parents from all sides of life. It's a philosophy. Heartfelt honesty and humor go a long way.

Fuck. That sounds like a hippy movement.

The first stage of your quest is to create your path and master the tools you need to function in your new normal. That new normal probably won't be what you imagined it to be. Maybe it will. What matters is that you choose what works for *your* family unit. Not your friend's or your sister's or your cousin's. Yours.

Remember that it can all change at a moment's notice, so appreciate the moments you have. Unless you're talking to Aunt Bertha, at which point, it might be time to practice asking for what you need, which is for her to put another cupcake in her mouth and cut the lecture.

You've embarked upon a quest that will be hard at times, brilliantly funny at other times, and heart-crushingly sad at others. You'll conquer fears and create new ones. You'll conquer mishaps from your childhood right before you watch your kid fall down the stairs and crack a tooth. You'll create beautiful memories to cherish for the rest of your life, only to have them topped off by your watch being flushed down the toilet, flooding the bathroom, and creating a mold problem for the neighbors who live underneath you.

Through it all, keep your chin up. This is life. It's not some app built by some socially awkward, fearful techie who never learned how to take the good with the bad. It's not a dense argument of graphs or stats, or a well-planned book of jargon that never works when you need it to. It's not a competition, because there are no awards for being a parent.

It's none of that. It's a blank canvas that you get to fill with the colors of life. That's what makes it valuable. After all, who wants to fill their home with shitty reproductions?

Maybe you're new to looking at life that way and this is hard. You'll get there. Be kind to yourself. One day you'll open your eyes, and your life will be staring back at you, and it will be so much more than you ever dreamed of. If it isn't like that right now, don't fret—the hard moments always pass.

Your quest is worth it. Enjoy the ride. It will be over before you know it. Though you won't believe that when you're five weeks in and haven't had a wink of sleep.

By the way. Welcome to your new Playground Mafia. We're happy to have you.

Good Luck

Made in the USA
Middletown, DE
02 August 2021